Essential England

AAA Publishing 1000 AAA Drive, Heathrow, Florida 32746

England: Regions and Best places to see

★ Best places to see 34–55

■ Featured sight

London 77–96

Northern England 97–116

Central England 117–140

Southeast England 141–164

Southwest England 165–187

Original text by Terry Marsh
Updated by Tim Locke

American editor: G.K. Sharman

Edited, designed and produced by AA Publishing, a trading name of AA Media Limited, whose registered address office is Fanum House, Basing View, Basingstoke, Hampshire RG21 4EA, UK. Registered number 06112600

Published in the United States by AAA Publishing,
1000 AAA Drive, Heathrow, Florida 32746
Published in the United Kingdom by AA Publishing

ISBN: 978-1-59508-368-5

Color separation: MRM Graphics Ltd
Printed and bound in Italy by Printer Trento S.r.l.

About this book

Symbols are used to denote the following categories:

➕ map reference to maps on cover

✉ address or location

☎ telephone number

🕐 opening times

🖐 admission charge

🍴 restaurant or café on premises
   or nearby

Ⓜ nearest underground train station

🚌 nearest bus/tram route

🚃 nearest overground train station

⛴ nearest ferry stop

✈ nearest airport

❓ other practical information

ℹ tourist information office

➤ indicates the page where you will
   find a fuller description

This book is divided into five sections.

The essence of England pages 6–19
Introduction; Features; Food and drink;
Short break including the 12 Essentials

Planning pages 20–33
Before you go; Getting there; Getting
around; Being there

Best places to see pages 34–55
The unmissable highlights of any visit
to England

Best things to do pages 56–73
Good places to have lunch; where to
take the children; best houses and
gardens; top outdoor activities; best
places to stay and more

Exploring pages 74–186
The best places to visit in England,
organized by area

Maps
All map references are to the maps on
the covers. For example, Oxford has the
reference ➕ P15 – indicating the grid
square in which it is to be found

Admission prices
Inexpensive (under £5)
Moderate (£5 and under £10)
Expensive (£10–£15)
Very expensive (over £15)

Hotel prices
Prices are per room per night: **£** budget
(under £70); **££** moderate (£70–£150);
£££ expensive to luxury (over £150)

Restaurant prices
Price for a three-course meal per person
without drinks: **£** budget (under £20);
££ moderate (£20–£30); **£££** expensive
(over £30)

Contents

THE ESSENCE OF...

6 – 19

PLANNING

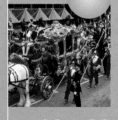

20 – 33

BEST PLACES TO SEE

34 – 55

BEST THINGS TO DO

56 – 73

EXPLORING...

74 – 186

The essence of...

Introduction   8–9

Features   10–11

Food and drink   12–15

Short break   16–19

England really is a green and pleasant land, a place of rolling landscapes and scenery that can make your heart ache. But it's also a varied and very cosmopolitan country, and offers so much that it is almost folly to try to cram everything into one visit (you simply won't). The secret is not to be too hasty. Linger, perhaps longer than you intended, whenever a particular place captures your imagination. Be flexible, change your plans as you go along, and be prepared to spend time exploring street markets, go for a walk in a town park, or simply enjoy a pint of beer at the local pub.

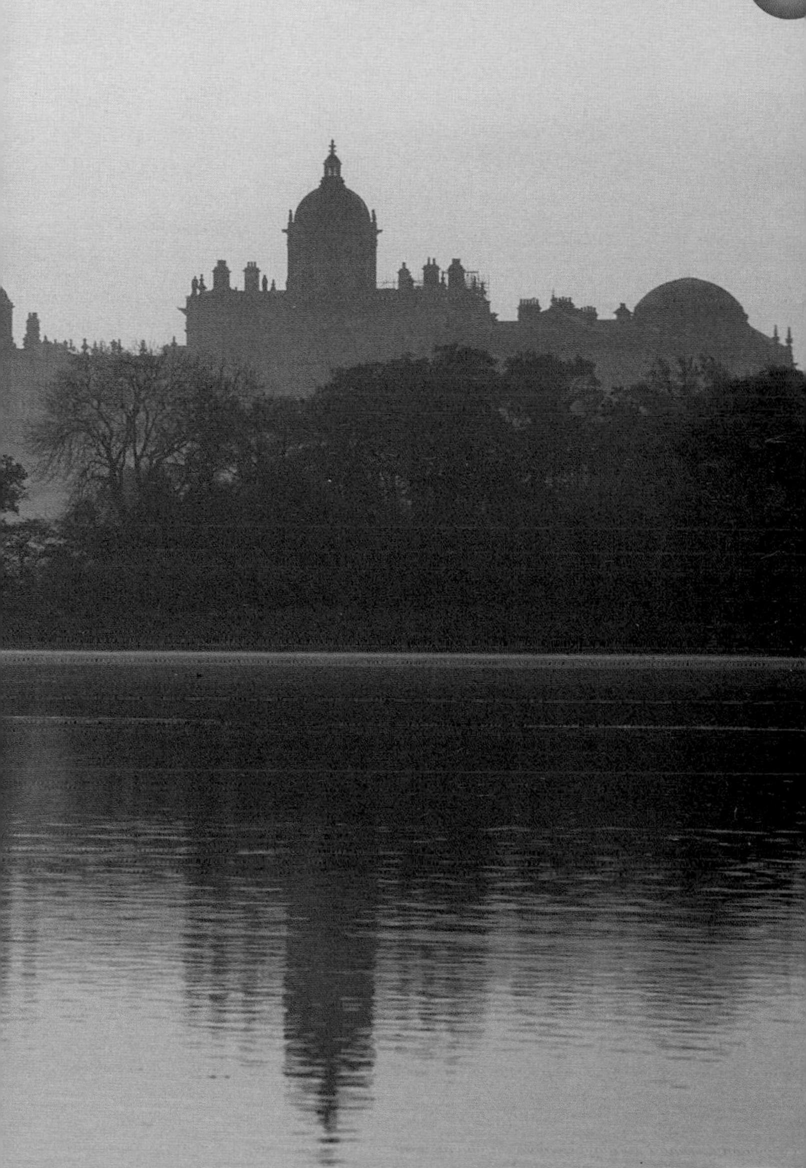

features

For many visitors it is hard to comprehend the variety England has to offer, from its charming country villages to the magnificent monuments of its great cities; it's a place of extremes but also seems very homogeneous and united.

Today England is a world leader in art, music and fashion. Politically and economically it is still a major player, as a part of the United Kingdom. There is a great feeling of openness, of a willingness to share England's heritage, whatever form it takes, with visitors and local people alike.

But England is also very European, in spite of the political bickering that goes on. Gone is the arrogance of imperialism; instead there is a recognition that England is one among many on the world's stage, with a role for everyone. It is a more worldly, more enterprising place that above all has a developing pride in its history and its place in the world.

THE COUNTRY

- England is the largest political division of the United Kingdom of Great Britain and Northern Ireland.
- It is a highly industrialized and agriculturally developed country, which is densely populated and rich in history.
- London, the capital, is also by far England's largest city, with over 7 million inhabitants.
- Birmingham in central England, the next largest city, has around a million inhabitants.

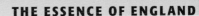

● Northern England boasts a clutch of cities with around 500,000 inhabitants, including Leeds, Manchester, Liverpool, Bradford, Sheffield and Newcastle. In the southwest, Bristol and Plymouth are the largest centres of population.

THE ECONOMY
● England's most important exports are oil, gas, technology and financial services.
● London's hosting of the 2012 Olympic Games should provide a welcome boost to the economy.

A FEW FACTS AND FIGURES
Area: 50,331sq miles (130,357sq km)
Currency: pound (£) sterling
Population: approx 50 million in 2008
Language: English, with many varied dialects. Several hundred minority languages also spoken.

OPEN SPACES
● In England, ten National Parks, including the newest in the New Forest, offer almost 5,000sq miles (13,000sq km) of countryside, protected for their scenic and recreational value.
● There are also more than 40 designated Areas of Outstanding Natural Beauty (AONB), with a similar protected status.
● Spread across the English countryside is a massive network of thousands of miles of footpaths, bridleways (open to horses and cyclists) and byways.
● Most towns and cities have formal parks in or near their centres, while in the surrounding areas you'll find country parks, where there is a less formal environment, and a greater chance of seeing some wildlife.

food & drink

It is virtually impossible to identify an English cuisine in the way that you might a French style – yet if such a thing exists, it is probably associated with good, plain cooking of fresh ingredients. In the mid-20th century it became characterized as 'meat and two veg' or 'school dinners', a sometimes affectionate reflection on the fare served up in school dining halls.

Come in for
A GOOD POT OF TEA
AND
Try Our
**CREAM TEAS
& CRAB SANDWICHES**

For many, 'English' means hearty meat pies, soggy vegetables and heavy desserts such as bread-and-butter-pudding, inevitably served with custard. In recent years 'modern English' has taken a lighter look at the old favourites, and you'll find new takes on traditional menus in pubs and restaurants across the country. And don't forget the sandwich was an English invention.

CHEESE

Cheeses are perhaps the most readily identifiable regional specialities. Cheddar (originally from Somerset) is the dominant style, but avoid the plastic supermarket variety and seek out the traditionally made from somewhere like Chewton Dairy in the Mendip Hills. Cheshire, Lancashire and Wensleydale are crumbly white cheeses, the prefix 'tasty' often used to

describe sharper, more mature varieties. They go very well with fruitcake. Central England produces the orangey-coloured Red Leicester, the smooth and herby Sage Derby and, most famously, the mature, blue-veined Stilton (delicious with a crisp apple). You'll find the best ranges of cheese are available at specialist delicatessens and farm stalls in traditional markets.

MEAT AND FISH

When it comes to meat, England is usually associated with beef, whether grilled as steak, roasted as a joint and served with Yorkshire pudding (savoury batter), or cooked slowly with root vegetables in a stew. Look for local speciality sausages; Cumberland are long and spicy, Lincolnshire, mild and herb flavoured. Black pudding, made with offal, is popular in the northern counties. Lamb too, is a popular ingredient but vegetarian food is also well established.

As you might expect, seafood is important. On the east coast, Craster is famous for its smoked kippers and Whitby for its crabs. In the

southeast, whelks, jellied eels, cockles and mussels are all popular. Wherever you are in England, you're never far from a fish and chip shop, selling cod or haddock fried in batter and served with chips. They're best eaten straight from the wrapper, and sprinkled with salt and vinegar.

CAKES AND ALE

Teatime may no longer be *the* afternoon event, but many English retain a fondness for cakes. A Lancashire Eccles cake is sweet mincemeat wrapped in pastry; gingerbread in Grasmere, Cumbria is a delicious, thin, crumbly affair more like a biscuit; and Derbyshire's Bakewell Pudding is commonly recognized as a jam tart topped with sponge cake.

There are English wines, though the climate means only the whites are generally up to world standards. In beers, you will find the global brands available alongside the peculiarly English ales. Served in pint glasses, the best of these are the 'real ales', which continue to mature in their barrels after leaving the brewery. The dominant varieties are bitters, such as Adnams or Greene King, but there are also numerous seasonal brews. Cider, a fermented apple drink, is normally stronger than beer, and has made a recent comeback, though still 'farm ciders' are found mostly in the southwest and western Midlands.

short break

If you have only a short time to visit England and would like to take home some unforgettable memories, you can do something local to capture the real flavour of the country. The following suggestions are a wide range of sights and experiences that won't take very long, won't cost too much and will make your visit very special.

● **Take a ride in a London cab** – ask the cabbie to show you as many of the sights of London as he can in an hour. Avoid rush hours and try fixing a price first.

● **Try real ale** or cider, particularly in a traditional English pub, where you can often find interesting beers from independent local breweries.

● **Visit a cathedral** – every one is an architectural marvel, and a peaceful place where you can slow things down for a while.

● **Watch a traditional ceremony.** Changing the Guard is the most famous daily event in London.

● **Explore the Lake District** – there is so much beautiful countryside in England, but the Lake District crams a lot in a small space (➤ 44–45).

● **Try fish and chips** – not really the English staple diet, but very filling.

● **Visit a stately home** – found all over the country, but allow enough time to see everything.

● **Go shopping in a street market** – markets are a traditional feature of many English towns. Increasing in popularity, even in cities, are farmers' markets which often sell organic and local produce. Check local press for details. Whether you buy anything or not, you're sure to be entertained by the market traders' banter.

● **Go to a show in London.** Try theatre box offices first or legitimate ticket agents such as Ticketmaster (www.ticketmaster.co.uk). Discounted tickets for same day performances can also be bought at the offical booths in Leicester Square and Brent Cross.

● **Watch a Premier League football match** – either at a stadium, or on the big TV with a pint of beer in a local pub.

● **Visit a village fête or agricultural show** – always a great day out, with cattle shows, dog trials, folk dancing, cookery competitions, craft displays and activities for the whole family.

● **Visit an industrial museum** – there are many around the country, but the Ironbridge Gorge (➤ 124–125) in Shropshire is looked on as the cradle of the Industrial Revolution.

Planning

Before you go   22–25

Getting there   26–27

Getting around   28–29

Being there   30–33

Before you go

WHEN TO GO

JAN	FEB	MAR	APR	MAY	JUN	JUL	AUG	SEP	OCT	NOV	DEC
6°C	7°C	10°C	13°C	17°C	20°C	22°C	22°C	19°C	14°C	10°C	7°C
43°F	45°F	50°F	55°F	63°F	68°F	72°F	72°F	66°F	57°F	50°F	45°F

High season   Low season

England is a destination with all-year-round appeal, but for the best weather, visit during the summer months (May to September). Daylight hours are longest in May and June, peaking at 17 hours daily. In the winter it gets dark at about 4pm. Thanks to a maritime climate, weather patterns across England are variable, but the Gulf Stream ensures that Britain is warmer than other countries on the same latitude, with temperatures rarely falling much below freezing in winter.

Although some attractions, such as many National Trust properties, close during the winter (typically from November to Easter), an off-peak visit should mean lower accommodation prices (outside the cities) and less-crowded sights.

WHAT YOU NEED

		UK	Germany	USA	Netherlands	Spain
●	Required					
○	Suggested					
▲	Not required					

Some countries require a passport to remain valid for a minimum period (usually at least six months) beyond the date of entry – contact their consulate or embassy or your travel agent for details.

	UK	Germany	USA	Netherlands	Spain
Passport (or National Identity Card where applicable)	▲	●	●	●	●
Visa (regulations can change – check before you travel)	▲	▲	▲	▲	▲
Onward or Return Ticket	▲	○	○	○	○
Health Inoculations (tetanus and polio)	▲	▲	▲	▲	▲
Health Documentation (➤ 23, Health Insurance)	▲	●	●	●	●
Travel Insurance	○	○	○	○	○
Driving Licence (national)	●	●	●	●	●
Car Insurance Certificate	▲	●	●	●	●
Car Registration Document	▲	●	●	●	●

WEBSITES

- www.visitbritain.com
- www.visitbritain.us
- www.english-heritage.org.uk
- www.enjoyengland.com
- www.bbc.co.uk
- www.thetrainline.com
- www.theaa.com
- www.nationalparks.gov.uk
- www.greatbritishgardens.co.uk
- www.fco.gov.uk
- www.metoffice.com
- www.nationaltrust.org.uk
- www.traveline.info
- www.artguide.org
- www.exhibitionsnet.com
- www.24hourmuseum.org.uk

TOURIST OFFICES AT HOME

In the UK

There are around 500 Tourist Information Centres in England, each independently run and staffed by local people. For details visit www.enjoyengland.com.

In the USA

Suite 701,
551 Fifth Avenue,
New York,
NY 10176
☎ 212/986-2266

HEALTH INSURANCE

The EHIC (European Health Insurance Card) allows EU nationals free or reduced cost medical treatment in other EU nations. It is free to apply for the card (www.ehic.org.uk). Private medical insurance is still advised, and is essential for all other visitors.

Emergency dental treatment may be available free of charge if you can find a National Health dentist willing to treat you. A list of dentists in the local area can be found in the Yellow Pages. Dental treatment should be covered by private medical insurance.

TIME DIFFERENCES

| GMT | British Summer | Germany | USA (NY) | Netherlands | Spain |
| 12 noon | 1PM | 1–2PM | 7AM | 1PM | 1PM |

England is on Greenwich Mean Time (GMT) in winter, but from late March until late October, British Summer Time (BST, i.e. GMT+1) operates.

NATIONAL HOLIDAYS

1 Jan *New Year's Day*
March/April *Good Friday and Easter Monday*
First Mon in May *May Day Bank Holiday*
Last Mon in May *Late May Bank Holiday*

Last Mon in August *August Bank Holiday Monday*
25 Dec *Christmas Day*
26 Dec *Boxing Day*

Almost all attractions close on Christmas Day. On other holidays some attractions open, often with reduced hours. There are no general rules regarding the opening times of restaurants and shops, so check before making a special journey.

WHAT'S ON WHEN

January or February *Chinese New Year* celebrations, Liverpool, Manchester and London.

March *Irish Festival*, Manchester.
Crufts Dog Show, NEC, Birmingham.

April *Oxford and Cambridge Boat Race*, River Thames, London. (Sometimes held in March.)
London Marathon, London.
Shakespeare's birthday, Stratford-upon-Avon, Warwickshire.

May *Furry Dance*, Helston, Cornwall.
Brighton Festival, Brighton, Sussex.
Obby Oss Festival, Padstow, Cornwall.
Bath International Music Festival, (late May to June), Bath, Somerset.
Royal Windsor Horse Show, Windsor Home Park.
Chelsea Flower Show, London.
Cheese Rolling Festival, Coopers Hill, Gloucestershire.

June *Trooping the Colour*, Horse Guards Parade, London.
Three Counties Show, Malvern, Worcestershire.
East of England Show, Peterborough, Cambridgeshire.
Wimbledon Tennis Championships, Wimbledon, London.
Appleby Horse Fair, Appleby-in-Westmorland, Cumbria.
Glastonbury Festival, Glastonbury, Somerset.

July *Farnborough International Airshow*, (even-numbered years) Hampshire.
Promenade Concerts ('Proms'), Royal Albert Hall, London (classical music concerts, until November).

The Great Yorkshire Show, Harrogate, Yorkshire.
Henley Royal Regatta, Henley-on-Thames, Oxfordshire.
Royal International Agricultural Show, Stoneleigh, Warwickshire.
Royal International Air Tattoo, Fairford, Gloucestershire.
August *International Beatles Week*, Liverpool.
Brighton Pride, Brighton, Sussex and *Manchester Pride,* Manchester.
Reading Festival, Reading, Berkshire.
Rush-bearing ceremony, Grasmere, Cumbria.
Southport Flower Show, Southport, Lancashire.
Billingham International Folklore Festival, Cleveland.
Notting Hill Carnival, London.
Grasmere Sports, Cumbria.
Cowes Regatta, Isle of Wight.
September *Artsfest*, Birmingham.
Blackpool Illuminations, Blackpool.
Southampton International Boat Show, Southampton, Hampshire.
Widecombe Fair, Widecombe-in-the-Moor, Devon.
October *Goose Fair*, Nottingham.
Great North Run, Gateshead.
London Film Festival, London.
World Conker Championships, Ashton, Northamptonshire.
November *Guy Fawkes Night* (firework displays throughout the country).
London to Brighton Veteran Car Run.
Lord Mayor's Show, London.
December *Frankfurt Christmas Market,* Birmingham.

Getting there

BY AIR

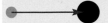

London Heathrow Airport

15.5 miles (25km) from city centre

60 minutes

40 minutes

40 minutes

London Gatwick Airport

30 miles (48km) from city centre

30 minutes

70–90 minutes

60–75 minutes

There are direct flights to England from all over the world. Most long-haul flights arrive at London Heathrow or London Gatwick, while London's other three airports (Stansted, Luton and London City) serve mainly short-haul destinations. International flights also operate from Birmingham International, Manchester, Southampton and Leeds–Bradford. Low-cost flights operate to some local airports.

BY SEA
Ferries serve England from Ireland and many ports in continental Europe. The 24-mile (38km) Channel Tunnel provides a fast train link with France via Eurostar (see below). The train service for cars, caravans and motorcycles through the tunnel is operated by Eurotunnel.

BY RAIL
Eurostar trains run beween St Pancras (London) and Ashford (Kent), in England; Paris and Lille, in France, and Brussels, in Belgium. Passports are required and passengers must clear customs before boarding.

DRIVING

- Drive on the left, overtake on the right.
- Speed limit on motorways and dual carriageways: 70mph (112kph)
  Speed limit on main roads: 50–60mph (80–96kph)
  Speed limit on minor roads: 30–40mph (48–65kph)
- Seat belts must be worn at all times.
- Random breath tests are carried out frequently, especially late at night. The limit is 35 micrograms of alcohol in 100ml of breath.
- Fuel is sold in litres and available as unleaded (95 octane), super unleaded (98 octane) and diesel. Other than in the centre of cities, fuel stations are numerous. The stations are typically open 6am–10pm (and 24 hours on major roads) but don't rely on these times in rural areas. Fuel is very heavily taxed, making it more expensive than in Europe or the USA. Prices vary slightly across the country.
- If you break down driving your own car and are a member of the AAA, you can call the AA (tel: 0800 887 766 toll free). If your car is rented, follow the instructions given in the documentation; most rental firms provide a rescue service.

Getting around

PUBLIC TRANSPORT

Internal flights Although the full-priced air fares are often far more than travelling by land, you can get some bargain 'no-frills' domestic flights through airlines such as easyJet and Ryanair. Major British cities – Edinburgh, Glasgow, Cardiff, Belfast – are well served.

Trains All the major towns and cities are connected by fast and frequent services, but intermediate stations tend to be served only by slower ones. Train lines radiate from London, and 'cross-country' services between provincial cities can be more difficult. The complex nature of the rail system's privatization in the 1990s means that a variety of differing operators may run trains on the same routes. There is a rail enquiry line and website to help you plan your journey (tel: 0845 748 4950; www.nationalrail.co.uk) and tickets can be bought in advance and over the

phone. Tickets are much more expensive if you leave it until your day of travel to buy them and if you travel during rush hour.

Buses These come in all shapes and sizes, providing cheap and effective local transport, either in urban areas or connecting small towns and villages in rural areas.

Coaches Travel by coach – a long-distance 'bus', and invariably more comfortable – is slower than train travel, but its relative cheapness makes it popular with the budget traveller. The main provider is National Express (www.nationalexpress.com) which serves most towns and cities.

CAR RENTAL

The leading international car rental companies have offices at all airports and you can book a car in advance. Local companies offer competitive rates and will deliver a car to the airport.

TAXIS

Anywhere in England you can telephone a private taxi company to collect you from where you are and take you to wherever you want to go. Your taxi may be any type of car, though London's famous 'black cabs' are increasingly found in other towns and cities.

FARES AND TICKETS

Children Those under 16 travel for half fare on public transport, and under 5s go free.

Railcards For reduced fares on most off-peak rail services, you can buy a Senior Railcard, Family and Friends Railcard, Disabled Person's Railcard or 16–25 Railcard, depending on your age and status. See www.railcard.co.uk.

BritRail Pass Available only to those living outside the UK, this gives unlimited travel for a given number of days over a given period; see www.britrail.com.

OysterCard For travelling in London, you will save money with an OysterCard. See www.tfl.gov.uk/oyster for more details.

Being there

TOURIST OFFICES

East Midlands Tourism
www.enjoyenglands
eastmidlands.com

Visit East of England
www.visiteastofengland.com

Visit England's Northwest
www.visitenglandsnorthwest.com

Visit the Heart of England
www.visittheheart.co.uk

Visit London
www.visitlondon.com

Visit North East England
www.visitnortheastengland.com

Tourism South East
www.visitsoutheastengland.com
☎ 023 8062 5400

South West Tourism
www.westcountrynow.com
☎ 0870 442 0880

Yorkshire Tourist Board
www.yorkshirevisitor.com

Additionally, many towns have a tourist information centre (TIC), signposted with an *i* symbol, with accommodation booking services.

MONEY

Britain's currency is the pound (£), issued in notes of £5, £10, £20 and £50. There are 100 pennies or pence (p) to each pound and coins come in denominations of 1p, 2p, 5p, 10p, 20p, 50p, £1 and £2. Travellers' cheques may be accepted by some hotels, shops and restaurants.

There are bureaux de change in most major streets in cities and towns, as well as at airports, rail stations and Underground stations in central London. Rates vary, and may be higher than at banks. Commission rates should be clearly displayed.

Credit and debit cards are accepted almost everywhere. They can also

TIPS/GRATUITIES

Yes ✓ No ✗		
Restaurants (if service not included)	✓	10–15%
Cafés/bars	✗	
Taxis	✓	10% or round up
Porters	✓	£1/bag
Chambermaids	✓	50p–£1per day
Cloakroom attendants	✓	loose change
Toilets	✗	

be used for drawing money at cashpoints (ATMs), where you pay a fixed withdrawal fee; debit cards may not incur a fee (check with your bank).

POSTAL AND INTERNET SERVICES

Post offices tend to be open Mon–Fri 9–5:30, Sat 9–1, though there are local variations.

Free wireless internet zones exist at many city locations such as stations and airports, as well as some city-centre coffee shops. Most public libraries have free internet access, though sometimes you have to reserve a time slot.

TELEPHONES

Traditional red phone boxes are now rare; instead, kiosks come in a wide variety of designs, depending on which phone company is operating them. Pay phones are either coin-operated and take 10p, 20p, 50p and £1 coins and some take credit cards. Other phone booths use prepaid cards which are readily available in shops. To call the operator dial 100.

Emergency telephone numbers
Police: 999　　　　　　　　**Ambulance:** 999
Fire: 999

International dialling codes
From England to:
Germany: 00 49　　　　　　**Netherlands:** 00 31
USA/Canada: 00 1　　　　　**Spain:** 00 34
Australia: 00 61

EMBASSIES AND CONSULATES
Germany ☎ 020 7824 1300　　**Netherlands** ☎ 020 7590 3200
USA ☎ 020 7499 9000　　　　**Spain** ☎ 020 7235 5555

ELECTRICITY
The power supply in Britain is 240 volts. Sockets only accept three (square)-pin plugs, so an adaptor is needed for Continental and US appliances. A transformer is needed for appliances operating on 110–120 volts.

HEALTH AND SAFETY

Drugs/medication Prescription and non-prescription drugs and medicines are available from chemists/pharmacies. Pharmacists can also advise on medication for common ailments. Chemists operate a roster so there will always be one that is open 24 hours; notices in all pharmacy windows give details.

Safe water Tap water is safe to drink. Mineral water is widely available but is often expensive, particularly in restaurants.

Personal safety The cities, towns and villages of England are all generally safe places to be. You will find the police force friendly, helpful and approachable.

To minimize the risk of personal crime:

- Don't carry more cash than you need and use the hotel safe or deposit boxes for storing valuables.
- Beware of pickpockets in markets and crowded places.
- Be alert in dark corners of cities late at night.

OPENING HOURS

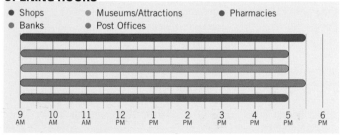

The times shown in the chart above are traditional opening hours. Many shops throughout England, especially those in the cities and large towns (but increasingly elsewhere) open for longer hours, many of them now on Sundays and bank holidays too for reduced hours. High Street banks are generally open Monday to Friday and Saturday mornings. Bureaux de change open daily. Museums and visitor attractions close for one day each week, and often on special occasions. It is best to check the times by telephoning in advance. When pharmacies are closed you'll find a sign in the window giving details of the nearest one that is open. Most post offices are closed on Saturday afternoons and all day Sunday.

LANGUAGE

The language spoken by the average English person is a far cry from the 'BBC English' (the kind spoken with perfect clarity and precision on national radio and television news). There are many strong regional accents. Norwich, Liverpool, Birmingham and Newcastle are all places with much idiosyncratic vocabulary. Don't worry if you don't understand the stronger variant accents – many English people don't either! The impact of greater social mobility and the expansion of metropolitan London into commuterland and 'overspill' towns has tended to blur the distinctions between accents in southeastern England, creating an amorphous linguistic derivative often called 'Estuarise' or 'Estuary English' after its origins along the Thames estuary. The English spoken by the English is noticeably different from that spoken by other English speakers in Australia or the USA for example. Below is a list of some of the obvious differences which can be confusing if you're not careful.

biscuit	*cookie or cracker*	jelly	*jello*
chips	*french fries*	off-licence	*liquor store*
crisps	*potato chips*	pudding	*dessert*
jam	*jelly*	sweets	*candy*
bonnet	*car hood*	petrol	*gasoline*
boot	*car trunk*	roundabout	*rotary*
caravan	*trailer*	road (surface)	*pavement*
car park	*parking lot*	return ticket	*round-trip ticket*
coach	*bus*	single ticket	*one-way ticket*
dual carriageway	*divided highway*	subway	*pedestrian*
lorry	*truck*		*passageway*
motorway	*highway*	underground	*subway*
bill	*check*	ground floor	*first floor*
busker	*street musician*	hire	*rent*
cheap	*inexpensive*	jumper	*sweater*
dustbin	*trash can*	leaflet	*pamphlet*
first floor	*second floor*	lift	*elevator*
football	*soccer*	pavement	*sidewalk*
fortnight	*two weeks*	trainers	*sneakers*

Best places to see

Bath	36–37
Cotswolds	38–39
Exmoor	40–41
Hadrian's Wall	42–43
Lake District	44–45
Oxford	46–47
Stonehenge	48–49
Tower of London	50–51
York	52–53
Yorkshire Dales	54–55

1 Bath

www.visitbath.co.uk

Bath is best known for its sweeping crescents of Georgian town houses and the remains of its Roman baths, now restored, in the centre of the city.

The Romans built a temple to the local water goddess Sulis here, and the first Bath spa (Aquae Sulis) was founded. The remains of the **Roman Baths** are among the most important in Europe, and heavily visited, being in the centre of town. Little survives from the Saxon and medieval towns which followed, though they were obviously of some importance. Edgar was crowned first king of all England here in 973.

The abbey church, completed in 1499, stands across an enclosed square

and contains some splendid vaulting. Aside from a heavily restored section of the old city walls, the rest of Bath is dominated by the changes wrought by leisure developers in the middle of the 18th century. Bath was then reinvented as the spa playground of the century's nouveaux riches. The Royal Crescent, Paragon, Circus and Lansdown Crescent were all magnificent streets built to accommodate the pleasure-seekers who came to Bath for the waters and the social scene. Walking is the best way to see the city, as the one-way traffic system can feel chaotic, but there are a number of open-top bus

tours which take in the less accessible sights.

Other sights include the **Fashion Museum** (housed in the Assembly Rooms, Cross Bath, Queen Square and Victoria Park) and the **American Museum of Decorative Art** at Claverton Manor.

➕ M16 ℹ️ Abbey Chambers ☎ 0906 711 2000

Roman Baths Museum

✉ Pump Room, Abbey Church Yard ☎ 01225 477785
🕐 Mar–Jun, Sep–Oct daily 9–5; Jul–Aug 9–9; rest of year 9:30–4:30 ✋ Expensive

Fashion Museum

✉ Bennett Street ☎ 01225 477789 🕐 Mar–Oct daily 10:30–5; Nov–Feb daily 10:30–4 ✋ Moderate

American Museum of Decorative Art

✉ Claverton Manor ☎ 01225 460503; www.americanmuseum.org 🕐 Mar–Oct and late Nov to mid-Dec Tue–Sun 12–5 ✋ Moderate

2 Cotswolds

The warmth of the honey-coloured stone villages and the rich green landscape make the Cotswolds one of England's most beautiful areas.

The Cotswold hills span six counties and roll gently between Bath in the south to Edge Hill in the north. On the western side the land drops away steeply above Stroud and Cheltenham, with superb views from hills such as Painswick Beacon and Cleeve Hill, and you can enjoy much of the best scenery by walking part of the Cotswold Way. The area has its own architectural style, seen in the mullioned windows and gables of its cottages and manor houses. Its long list of attractions features some of the finest gardens in the country.

The great parish churches and inns demonstrate the prosperity of the area which began in the late Middle Ages. Sheep farming underpinned this wealth and made a huge impact on the landscape as the Cotswolds became rich on wool and cloth. Chipping Campden, Northleach and Cirencester contain good examples of 'wool churches', heavily adorned with gargoyles.

The often overcrowded village of Broadway acts as a gateway to the region, with tourist shops and tearooms abounding. Bourton-on-the-Water is another tourist hotspot, with the River Windrush running pleasantly through its centre. Upper and Lower Slaughter attract visitors as much for their peculiar names as their chocolate-box looks.

You are able to get a better feel for the Cotswolds' charm in less-visited gems such as Stanton, Snowshill or Bibury. Arlington Row, a delightful terrace of former weavers' cottages in Bibury best epitomizes Cotswold village character.

✚ N15

ℹ Contact local tourist information offices for specific details.
Cheltenham office: ☎ 01242 522878;
www.visitcheltenham.gov.uk

3 Exmoor

www.visit-exmoor.co.uk

Sweeping heather moors are split by wooded valleys, or coombs, which tumble into the sea in this national park on the border of Somerset and Devon.

The mood changes from one moment to the next, with a rugged coast boasting some of the highest cliffs in England, and secretive forests, windswept moors, tranquil river valleys and sleepy villages. Exmoor does get quite a bit of rain, and there are no great beaches and few contrived tourist attractions: this is an area to enjoy being outdoors, and walking the coast path. You can drive close to the summit of Dunkery Beacon, at 1,702ft (519m) Exmoor's highest point, for huge views across the Bristol Channel to South Wales. Outstanding among its villages are Dunster, with its octagonal yarn market overlooked by a castle and a watermill preserved nearby; Selworthy, with its thatched cottages and wagon-roofed church; and Winsford,

with its many bridges. Spanning the Barle near Withypool, Tarr Steps is an ancient stone bridge believed to be 1,000 years old.

At the northern edge of the park the twin towns of Lynton and Lynmouth are linked by a 19th-century water-powered cliff railway. The lower town, at the mouth of the two Lyn rivers, was famously devastated by a flood in 1953. The upper town boasts fine views and leads to the

NATIONAL PARK
EXMOOR

spectacular, dry Valley of Rocks, running parallel to the dramatic 500ft (150m) coastal cliffs. Nearby Watersmeet is a popular beauty spot deep in a tree-lined ravine where Hoar Oak Water joins the East Lyn River. Among the wildlife found on Exmoor is the red deer, the stag's antlers making up the national park logo.

✚ K16 ✉ Exmoor National Park 7–9, Fore Street, Dulverton, Somerset ☎ 01398 323841

4 Hadrian's Wall

www.hadrians-wall.org

The purpose of this great Roman wall was 'to separate the Romans from the Barbarians' – *'qui barbaros Romanosque divideret...'*

One of a series of Roman boundary fortifications built right across northern Europe, Hadrian's Wall stretches for 73 miles (117km) between Wallsend, on the east coast near Newcastle upon Tyne, to Bowness-on-Solway in Cumbria on the west coast. Begun in AD122, the wall took six years to complete and is 10ft (3m) thick in places. The walkway which ran along the top was sometimes as high as 3.5m (12ft) above the ground.

The wall was built to protect Roman Britain from raiding Picts from what is now Scotland, and the most dramatic sections still run close to the Anglo-Scottish border. Hadrian's Wall was abandoned in AD383, and though much of the stone from the wall was used in local buildings, enough remains to give a vivid picture of a Roman frontier province. A World Heritage Site, the wall features many museums and interpretative centres along its length that portray life in Roman times, notably at Birdoswald, Once Brewed, Vindolanda and Chesters, but the best is the **Housesteads Fort and Museum.** Known to the Romans as Vercovicium, Housesteads is the most complete Roman fort in Britain, and occupies a spectacular position with commanding views across the bleak Northumbrian countryside. It was garrisoned by about 1,000 soldiers and the museum recreates aspects of their life as well as explaining the natural history of the region. Walkers can follow the course of the wall along a National Trail.

➕ C3
🛈 Wentworth car park, Hexham, Northumberland
☎ 01434 652220
Housesteads Fort and Museum
✉ Housesteads ☎ 01434 344363 🕓 Apr–Sep daily 10–6; Oct–Mar daily 10–4. Closed 1 Jan, 24–26 Dec
👆 Inexpensive

5 Lake District

www.lake-district.gov.uk

Few places in England have the richly varied landscape of the Lake District; fewer still its wealth of local history and legends.

The Lake District, in Cumbria in northwest England, has a special beauty all of its own: it is the largest and most spectacular of all the English national parks, with a series of lakes radiating from a central core of mountains (always known as 'fells' here). Part of its enduring appeal is due to its extraordinary variety, with the scenery changing dramatically from one valley to the next. It is all at a scale ideal for walking – from easy strolls along lake shores to demanding hikes along high ridges and scrambles up craggy slopes – though there is also a great range of sights and crafts shops for the area's many rainy days. On the east side is Windermere – England's longest lake, which you can explore by cruise boat – amid gentle, green hills and woodlands. Further west the land rises to the main fell group, which includes Helvellyn, Skiddaw and Great Gable: you can get magnificent views by venturing through Langdale and up the spectacular Wrynose and Hardknott passes into Eskdale, and then on to Wast Water, England's deepest lake, beneath Scafell Pike, England's highest mountain. North from there, the fells provide a majestic frame for the small lake of Buttermere, from where the Honister Pass leads on to the wooded craggy heights of Borrowdale. The antique steam yacht *Gondola* makes a memorable excursion on

Coniston Water, while there are also two steamers – *Lady of the Lake* and *Raven* – along the length of sinuous Ullswater in the northeast corner of the national park.

Of the principal tourist centres, the towns of Windermere, Bowness and Kendal attract thousands of day trippers and are easily accessible by road and rail. Many make for the **Visitor Centre** at Brockhole. Keswick, in the north, nestles amid towering fells beside Derwent Water and has a seemingly limitless supply of outdoor clothing shops. Ambleside, at the head of Windermere (lake), in the south, plays a similar role. Grasmere, with nearby Rydal, is between the two and famously associated with the poet William Wordsworth, a Cumbrian who did much of his best work while living here.

➕ B4

Lake District Visitor Centre

✉ Brockhole (on A591 between Windermere and Ambleside), Cumbria ☎ 01539 446601 ⏱ Mid-Feb to Oct daily 10–5. Grounds and gardens: daily ✋ Free. Pay and display car park: moderate (£6 all day)

6 Oxford

www.visitoxford.org

Oxford, familiar to many from the Inspector Morse stories, is striking for the physical beauty of its ancient university.

A delightful city to wander round at any time of year, Oxford has two particular treasures: the stunning heritage of historic buildings that make up the university, and the parks and leafy river walks. From Magdalen Bridge you can hire a punt and explore the river. As at Cambridge, there is no campus, but students live and study at colleges scattered around the city.

There has been educational influence in the city since at least 1167 when students expelled from

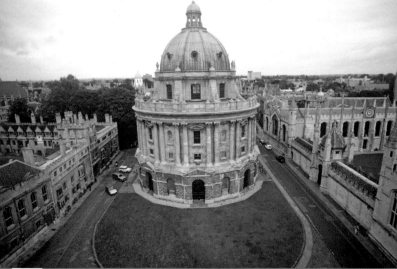

Paris settled here. The colleges, with their quadrangles, refectories and chapels, still reflect the religious houses upon which they were founded.

There are 36 colleges in all; some you can visit. Built mostly of golden Cotswold limestone, the colleges display a magnificent range of architectural styles, from the early Gothic of Merton College to the Victorian red-brick extravaganza of Keble. Christ Church, the grandest college, has a picture gallery, the biggest quad and a chapel that doubles as England's smallest cathedral.

Of outstanding interest is the **Ashmolean Museum,** England's oldest public museum, which was founded in 1683. It houses the University's enormous collections of art and antiquities. On the corner of Broad Street you'll also find the **Bodleian Library** and the Sheldonian Theatre.

✚ P15

ℹ️ 16 Broad Street ☎ 01865 726871 🕐 Mon–Sat 9:30–5 (Jul–Aug Thu–Sat 9:30–6), Sun 10–4

Ashmolean Museum

✉️ Beaumont Street ☎ 01865 278000; www.ashmolean.org 🕐 Tue–Sat and bank hols 10–5, Sun 12–5. Closed 1 Jan, Good Fri–Easter Sun, 3 days early Sep, 24–28 Dec 💷 Free ❓ Guided tours

Bodleian Library

✉️ Broad Street ☎ 01865 277224; www.shop.bodley. ox.ac.uk 🕐 Mon–Fri 9–5 (times may vary), Sat 9–1. Closed Easter and 25 Dec 💷 Inexpensive ❓ Guided tours: daily 10:30, 11:30, 2, 3

7 Stonehenge

www.english-heritage.org.uk/stonehenge

The great stone circle at Stonehenge is one of the wonders of the world, as old as many of the temples and pyramids of Egypt.

Stonehenge (from the Old English 'hanging stones') is 2 miles (3.2km) west of Amesbury in Wiltshire, and one of the best-known archaeological sites in the world. It is not, as might be supposed, an isolated monument. In reality, the stones are part of an extensive prehistoric landscape filled with the remains of ceremonial and domestic structures.

What you see today is the last in a series of monuments erected in several stages between 3000 and 1600BC. Each is circular in form and aligned along the rising of the sun at the midsummer solstice, though many of the structures are now incomplete.

Archaeologists still debate whether Stonehenge was a place of ritual sacrifice and sun worship, some kind of astronomical calculator, or a royal palace. But for thousands of years it was an important focal point within a ceremonial landscape. The structure also represents a massive investment in time and human resources. Enormous effort was needed to transport the stones, some weighing up to 40 tons, from sites tens or hundreds of miles away, notably from Preseli in Wales, from where they must have been dragged or floated on rafts.

Stonehenge is now a UNESCO World Heritage Site, and although conflict has arisen between modern druids, new-age travellers and the police over access to the site, there is no doubt that its conservation has been taken very seriously. There are recommended walks exploring the surrounding downland of Salisbury Plain and an archaeological leaflet available from the gift shop to help you interpret this ancient landscape.

✚ N16 ✉ Near Amesbury, Wiltshire ☎ 0870 333 1181
🕐 Mid-Mar to May, Sep to mid-Oct daily 9:30–6; Jun–Aug daily 9–7; mid-Oct to mid-Mar daily 9:30–4; 26 Dec and 1 Jan 10–4. Closed 24–25 Dec 🖐 Moderate 🍴 Stonehenge Kitchen (£–££) ❓ Self-guided audio tours

8 Tower of London

www. hrp.org.uk

Overlooking the Thames, the Tower of London is famous as a place of imprisonment and death; it's also one of England's foremost medieval fortresses.

The Tower, not just one tower but a whole castle-full, is one of London's great landmarks. It has been

ENTRY TO THE TRAITORS GATE

a royal residence, an armoury and the home, as it still is, of the Crown Jewels. It is surrounded by Tower Green, where the executions of two of Henry VIII's wives (Anne Boleyn and Catherine Howard) took place. Here you'll find two of the Tower's famous ravens, the latest in a long line protected by royal decree. Their wings are clipped to stop them flying away, for should they leave, legend claims the Tower and kingdom will fall.

Walks around the Tower are conducted by Yeoman Warders (Beefeaters), who recount tales of torture and intrigue.

The Crown Jewels are housed in the Jewel House. Viewing them is a rather hurried affair as visitors are carried along moving walkways. Among the dazzling display is the Imperial State Crown which contains a 317-carat diamond, sapphires, emeralds, rubies and pearls, but the most famous of the diamonds is the Koh-i-Noor, set into a crown made for the Queen Mother in 1937.

In the Bloody Tower are the rooms where the 'Princes in the Tower', the 12-year-old Edward V and his brother Richard, were supposedly murdered by Richard III and where Sir Walter Raleigh was held captive for 13 years.

✚ *London h2 (off map)* ☎ 0870 756 6060 ❸ Mar–Oct Tue–Sat 9–5:30, Sun–Mon 10–5:30; Nov–Feb Tue–Sat 9–4:30, Sun–Mon 10–4:30. Last admission 30 mins before closing. Closed 1 Jan, 24–26 Dec ✋ Very expensive 🍴 Café (£) Ⓣ Tower Hill 🚌 15, 42, 78, 100, RV1 🚆 Fenchurch Street (National Rail); Tower Gateway (DLR) ❓ Buy tickets in advance from any underground Travel Information Centre. Free hour-long tours run every half hour

York

www.visityork.org

York is one of the few cities in England that still feels medieval. Begun by the Romans in AD71, it became an important city, which they called Eboracum.

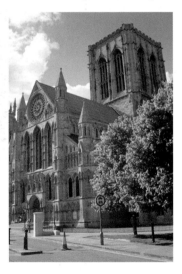

'York' comes from the Scandanavian *Jorvik*, and the **Jorvik Viking Centre** in Coppergate houses a vivid display of York under Scandanavian domination. Later, the Normans made York their centre of government, commerce and religion in the north. Taking centre stage is the magnificent Minster, which took 250 years to build and was completed and consecrated in 1472. Now one of the city's essential visitor attractions, it contains England's finest collection of medieval stained glass.

During the Middle Ages, York was an important wool-trading centre. On the prosperity of this trade rode the success of other tradespeople, notably goldsmiths, butchers, shoemakers and saddlers, who came to live in the city. Many of these traders lived in Stonegate, Goodramgate and the Shambles, streets which are still very medieval in

appearance; the modern shops here are shaped around the plots laid out over 1,000 years ago.

The medieval city walls are also largely intact and make an interesting circular walk of around 2.5 miles (4km). Beyond the walls, the **National Railway Museum** is the keeper of Britain's railway heritage and is well worth visiting for its huge displays from the golden age of steam.

✚ D6 ℹ️ De Grey rooms, Exhibition Square
☎ 01904 550099 🕐 Mon–Sat 9–6, Sun 10–5; winter Mon–Sat 10–5, Sun 10–4

Jorvik Viking Centre
✉ Coppergate ☎ 01904 643211; www.jorvik-viking-centre.co.uk 🕐 Daily 10–5 ✋ Expensive

National Railway Museum
✉ Leeman Road ☎ 08448 153139; www.nrm.org.uk
🕐 Daily 10–6 ✋ Free

10 Yorkshire Dales

www.yorkshiredales.org.uk

A series of charming upland valleys, each with a distinctive character, makes up this popular national park.

Lying astride the Pennines in the north of England, the Yorkshire Dales are a popular area of rugged moorlands, rivers, streams (here called becks and valleys – the 'dales'), patterned by hedgerows, drystone walls and villages. The principal dales – Airedale, Wharfedale, Nidderdale, Wensleydale and Swaledale – have a distinctive character and culture and noticeably different dialects. But the landscape unites them, with its open fells, heather moors, limestone crags and close-cropped turf.

The region is honeycombed with cave systems so complex that some remain unexplored. There are show caves at Clapham and near Grassington. Grassington itself, a delightful village around a small square in Wharfedale, has a fine museum of Dales life. Nearby Bolton Priory is a medieval abbey picturesquely situated in meadowland, surrounded by woods and rolling moorland. Airedale's biggest attraction is Malham Cove, a huge 250ft (76m) inland cliff which dominates the head of the valley. Wensleydale, famous for its cheese, lies further

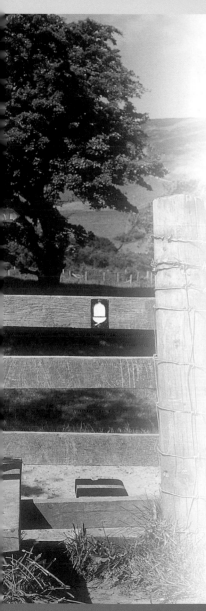

north and boasts several spectacular waterfalls as well as the busy little market town of Hawes. Swaledale is altogether more remote and wild, its northern fringe sloping off into the high moorlands of the north Pennines. Lead mining was very important here until the end of the 19th century and the area's gills (side valleys) bear the healed scars of this industry.

The surrounding towns such as Settle and Ingleton in the west, Skipton (➤ 112–113) in the south and Richmond (➤ 111) and Leyburn in the east make excellent centres for exploration. This is splendid walking country: highlights include the waterfalls at Ingleton, the ascents of Ingleborough and Pen-y-ghent, from Malham to Gordale Scar, the Pennine Way between Muker and Keld in Swaledale, and strolls to such beauty spots as Aysgarth Falls and Hardraw Force in Wensleydale.

➕ C5 ✉ Yorkshire Dales National Park Centre, Grassington ☎ 01756 751694; www.yorkshirevisitor.com ⏰ Apr–Oct daily 10–5; Nov–Mar Sat–Sun 10–4 only

Best things to do

Good places to have lunch   58–59

Places to take the children   60–61

Good pubs   62–63

Best houses and gardens   64–65

Top outdoor activities   66–67

A walk through London's royal
parks   68–69

Best walks   70–71

Best places to stay   72–73

Good places to have lunch

Antony's (££–£££)

Accolades have been heaped upon this father-and-son-run restaurant, which opened in 2004. The set lunch is a bargain introduction to their adventurous, world-class cooking.

✉ 19 Boar Lane, Leeds ☎ 0113 245 5922; www.anthonysrestaurant.co.uk

The Glass House (££)

Restored mill building with huge windows. Contemporary Mediterranean dishes alongside traditional British food.

✉ Rydal Road, Ambleside, Cumbria ☎ 01539 432137; www.theglasshouserestaurant.co.uk

Green's Café (£)

A varied selection of sandwiches, paninis, organic and fair-trade food, salads and other light meals are on offer here, along with free WiFi for laptop users.

✉ 50 St Giles, Oxford ☎ 01865 316878

The Jolly Sportsman (£–££)

Marvellous beers are served at this word-of-mouth gastropub and the food is equally enticing, with seafood a speciality.

✉ Chapel Lane, East Chiltington, East Sussex ☎ 01273 890400; www.thejollysportsman.co.uk

Number Twelve (£–££)

Modern Italian food superbly presented, within a stylishly remodelled hotel near Euston; the short lunch menu is great value.

✉ Ambassadors Bloomsbury Hotel, 12 Upper Woburn Place, London ☎ 020 7693 5425

The Old Success Inn (£–££)

A fishing inn dating from the 17th century, serving home-made specials, seafood and sandwiches.

✉ Sennen Cove, Cornwall ☎ 01736 871232

Pump Room (££)

Be serenaded by musicians as you have lunch or sip afternoon tea at this Georgian pump room.

✉ Abbey Church Yard, Bath ☎ 01225 444477

The Refectory (£)

Good coffee and light snacks served in the atmospheric cloisters.

✉ Cathedral Cloisters, Wells, Somerset ☎ 01749 676543

Tate Britain Rex Whistler Restaurant (££)

Rex Whistler's murals here provide the backdrop to unfussy food.

✉ Millbank, London ☎ 020 7887 8825; www.tate.org.uk/britain/eatanddrink/restaurant

Places to take the children

The Animal Ark and Country Park

Plenty of opportunities to meet, cuddle and feed a wide range of wild and domestic animals, go trampolining or try the go-karts.

✉ Great Witchingham, Norfolk ☎ 01603 872274; www.theanimalark.org
🕓 Mid-Mar to Oct daily 10–5 🖐 Moderate

Eureka!

Award-winning hands-on museum of science designed especially for children.

✉ Discovery Road, Halifax, West Yorkshire ☎ 01422 330069;
www.eureka.org.uk 🕓 Daily 10–5. Closed 24–26 Dec 🖐 Moderate

The Flambards Experience

Family attraction including Victorian village, rides, aviation display, science centre and wartime displays.

✉ Culdrose Manor, Helston, Cornwall ☎ 01326 573404;
www.flambards.co.uk 🕓 Apr–Oct daily 10:30–5; Nov–Mar daily 11–4
🖐 Expensive (includes all rides and entertainment)

Ironbridge Gorge Museums

The world's first iron bridge was cast and built here in 1779. Now the site of a splendid series of ten historical industrial museums and exhibitions that are endlessly fascinating (► 124–125).

✉ Ironbridge, Telford, Shropshire ☎ 01952 884391; www.ironbridge.org.uk
🕓 Daily 10–5. Some museums closed Nov–Mar 🖐 Moderate–expensive;
ask about a passport to all museums

Legoland Windsor

This gloriously landscaped theme park in miniature is dedicated to the imagination and creativity of children. It was specifically designed for the under-12s and will easily keep the kids amused for a day.

✉ Windsor Park, Windsor, Berkshire ☎ 0871 2222 001; www.legoland.co.uk
🕓 Mar–Oct most days; see website or phone for details 🖐 Very expensive

Madame Tussaud's

World leaders, musicians, athletes and film actors stand side by side in this legendary exhibition of wax figures in London.

✉ Marylebone Road, London
☎ 0870 999 0046;
www.madame-tussauds.co.uk
🕐 Mon–Fri 9:30–5:30, Sat–Sun 9–6 ✋ Very expensive
🚇 Baker Street

Magna

Science adventure centre exploring earth, air, fire, water and power with lots of hands-on, interactive challenges. There are four adventure pavilions, an outdoor adventure park and an outdoor wet area.

✉ Sheffield Road, Templeborough, Rotherham ☎ 01709 720002; www.visitmagna.co.uk 🕐 Daily 10–5. Closed 24–25 Dec ✋ Expensive

National Maritime Museum

Britain's seafaring history; the world of Nelson and the glory of the British Empire; 20th-century seapower and luxury liners.

✉ Romney Road, Greenwich, London ☎ 020 8858 4422, www.nmm.ac.uk
🕐 Daily 10–5 ✋ Free 🚇 DLR: Cutty Sark

Speedwell Cavern

Go down 105 steps to a boat that takes you more than a mile (1.5km) through underground, water-filled caverns.

✉ Winnats Pass, Castleton, Derbyshire ☎ 01433 620512; www.speedwellcavern.co.uk 🕐 Mon–Fri 10–4 ✋ Moderate

Good pubs

Bell
In the quiet street of a Cotswold village, with outstanding food and a good choice of local real ales. There's a range of comfortable sitting places in cosy beamed rooms or outside.
✉ Sapperton, Gloucestershire ☎ 01285 760298

The Britannia Inn
Everything you would expect from a traditional British inn. The Britannia stands next to a village green with an ancient maple tree.
✉ Elterwater, Cumbria ☎ 01539 437210

The George of Stamford
A stylish and busy old coaching inn built in 1597 for Lord Burghley, who was a statesman and an advisor to Queen Elizabeth I.
✉ 71 St Martin's, Stamford, Lincolnshire ☎ 01780 750750

Harrow Inn

Tucked away down a sleepy lane, this excellent, unspoiled country pub has been run by the same family since 1929.

✉ Steep, Hampshire ☎ 01730 262685

The New Inn

An early 17th-century, ivy-covered stone pub that is becoming especially popular for its imaginative blackboard 'specials' available daily. Games include chess and dominoes.

✉ Yealand Conyers, Lancashire ☎ 01524 732938

Pandora

Ancient thatched pub in a lovely waterside position. Enjoy tasty bar food in the flagstoned, low-ceilinged rooms.

✉ Mylor Bridge, Cornwall ☎ 01326 372678

Red Lion

A delightfully traditional village pub in rural surroundings just west of London, the Red Lion has good value bar food, and pleasant walks in Chess Valley; no children inside.

✉ Chenies, Buckinghamshire ☎ 01923 282722

Three Chimneys

The candlelit restaurant is just the place to enjoy the accomplished cooking here, after a visit to the nearby gardens at Sissinghurst. Real ales and very good local cider.

✉ Biddenden, Kent ☎ 01580 291472

Three Horseshoes

A real time warp, with gas lighting, stone floor, open fires and a collection of wind-up gramophones: full of friendly chatter, and a nice place for beer, local cider and hearty bar food.

✉ Warham, Norfolk ☎ 01328 710547

Best houses and gardens

HOUSES
Audley End House
Fine Jacobean house with 30 rooms open to the public. Grounds landscaped by 18th-century landscape architect Lancelot 'Capability' Brown.

✉ Saffron Walden, Suffolk ☎ 01799 522399; www.english-heritage.org.uk /audleyend 🕐 Grounds: Apr–Sep Wed–Sun, 10–6; Oct and Mar 10–5; rest of year 10–4. House: mid-Mar to Sep Wed–Sun 11–5 (Sat 11–3:30); Oct Wed–Sun 11–4 👋 Expensive

Hampton Court Palace
Splendid Tudor palace on the River Thames; for centuries the home of British monarchs.

✉ Hampton Court, Surrey ☎ 0844 482 7777; www.hrp.org.uk 🕐 Daily 10–4:30 👋 Expensive

Hardwick Hall
Exceptional 16th-century house built for Bess of Hardwick with much of the original furnishings. Rare breeds in the huge park.

✉ Near Chesterfield, Derbyshire ☎ 01246 850430; www.nationaltrust.org.uk 🕐 Mar–Nov Wed–Thu, Sat–Sun 12–4:30; Dec Sat–Sun only 11–3; times may vary 👋 Expensive

Petworth House and Park
Unrivalled art collection, fine woodcarvings and a deer park.

✉ Petworth, West Sussex ☎ 01798 342207; www.nationaltrust.org.uk 🕐 Mid-Mar to Oct Sat–Wed 11–5 👋 Expensive. Park: free

GARDENS
Clumber Park
Huge country park encompassing forest, parkland, a lake and a walled kitchen garden (➤ 130). Special weekend events in summer.

✉ Worksop, Nottinghamshire ☎ 01909 544917; www.nationaltrust.org.uk ⏰ Daily dawn–dusk. Gardens. Apr–Sep daily 10–5; Oct 10–4 💷 Free. Gardens: inexpensive

Harlow Carr Botanical Garden
The Royal Horticultural Society's show garden in the north, with ornamental and woodland areas.

✉ Cragg Lane, Harrogate, North Yorkshire ☎ 01423 565418; www.rhs.org.uk ⏰ Mar–Oct daily 9:30–5; Nov–Feb daily 9:30–4 💷 Moderate

Lost Gardens of Heligan
Magnificent reclaimed gardens with jungle garden, pineapples in heated glasshouses, a crystal grotto, summerhouses and pools. The Productive Gardens have more than 300 varieties of fruit and vegetables.

✉ Pentewan, St Austell, Cornwall ☎ 01726 845100; www.heligan.com ⏰ Mar–Oct daily 10–6; Nov–Feb 10–5 💷 Moderate

Westonbirt Arboretum
One of Europe's largest and most diverse collections of trees and shrubs. Glorious displays year-round, especially in autumn.

✉ Near Tetbury, Gloucestershire ☎ 01666 880220; www.forestry.gov.uk/westonbirt ⏰ Daily 9–5 (Sun 10–5), or dusk if earlier 💷 Moderate

Top outdoor activities

Go to a football match. Although tickets may be hard to come by for the Premier League teams like Chelsea and Manchester United, you can usually get into matches in the lower divisions.

Go for a country walk in one of the national parks. Park information offices have leaflets about guided trails and wildlife.

Rent a boat and go rowing on a park lake or river. In Oxford or Cambridge, take out a punt, student-style.

Go horse-back riding. There are British Horse Society (BHS) approved riding schools in most areas. Tourist offices can supply details.

Walk a town trail – it's one of the best ways of getting to know a place: leaflets are usually available at the local tourist information centre.

Tour the country lanes on a rented bike – and take a picnic. For information on where to cycle see www.sustrans.org.uk.

Have a flutter at a horse race. There are racecourses all over the country. For more information, visit www.britishhorseracing.com.

Watch a county cricket match on a warm summer's day – the one-day game is probably the most entertaining.

Visit one of England's many ancient stone sites, such as Avebury in Wiltshire or Castlerigg in Cumbria.

a walk

through London's royal parks

The royal parks are wonderful oases of green in the very heart of London; this walk links four of them.

Begin from Westminster, opposite the Houses of Parliament. Cross Parliament Square and go into Great George Street. Take the first right, and turn into St James's Park.

St James's is the oldest and most attractive of the central London parks, established by Henry VIII in the 1530s.

Keep to the left of the lake until you can cross it by a bridge.

The views from the bridge are splendid in both directions: face the impressive buildings of Whitehall, and behind you lies Buckingham Palace.

Over the bridge, turn left, and go up to join The Mall. Cross The Mall and walk towards Buckingham Palace. Keep right, by the edge of Green Park, and up Constitution Hill. Tackle the Green Park and Hyde Park Corner pedestrian underpass as if going to Hyde Park station, but continue instead up to Hyde Park.

Hyde Park (➤ 81) originally belonged to the Church, until Henry VIII seized it to use as hunting grounds.

By keeping to the eastern side of the park you eventually find your way to Marble Arch. Go through the pedestrian underpass here, to exit 14 onto Oxford Street. Keep walking straight along Oxford Street until you can turn left onto Portman Street. Turn right into Portman Square and walk along until you reach the crossroads of Baker and Wigmore streets, turning left to walk along Baker Street and the other side of Portman Square. Continue along Baker Street for a short distance to reach Regent's Park. Return from Baker Street station.

Distance 4.25 miles (7km)
Time 3–4 hours including stops
Start point Houses of Parliament 🚇 *London d5*
End point Regent's Park 🚇 *London b1* (off map)
Lunch The Lido Café, in Hyde Park (£)

Best walks

Buttermere, Lake District

An easily managed 3-mile (4.8km) circuit of
this beautifully set lake from Buttermere
village goes to show that a walk doesn't
have to be tough to be magnificent. It's
almost level, close to the shore, with
stupendous views of the fells all around.

Land's End, Cornwall

The most majestic stretch of Cornwall's superb coastline
runs some 5.5 miles (9km) from the southwestern tip of
Land's End to Treen. Follow the strenuous coast path up
and down a series of headlands and bays, past the sandy
beach at Porthcurno to get the bus back from Treen.

Malham Cove, Yorkshire Dales

You need a map for this classic short walk, or you can find
leaflets from national park offices. The route from Malham
leads along the Pennine Way past Janet's Foss waterfall,
then on up to Gordale Scar waterfall. Carry on up to the
limestone pavement, above the top of Malham Cove.

Seven Sisters, East Sussex

Start at Seven Sisters Country
Park (trail leaflet available in visitor
centre). Follow the path to
Cuckmere Haven, then hike the
series of dizzying chalk cliffs known
as the Seven Sisters (▶ 155). For
an 8-mile (13km) walk, carry on
to Birling Gap and Belle Tout
Lighthouse, then head inland past
the village of East Dean and
through Friston Forest.

Symonds Yat, Herefordshire

Close to the Welsh border, Symonds Yat rock gives a spectacular view over a loop of the River Wye, which carves a route through a gorge deep below. From Symonds Yat car park, walk down to the river, where from the Saracens Head Inn, a ferryman takes you across on a chain ferry to the far bank. Follow the river downstream to the wire bridge, which bounces as you cross it, and return to the start (3.5 miles/5.5km).

Tennyson Down, Isle of Wight

The favourite walk of the Victorian poet Alfred Lord Tennyson, this glorious whaleback coastal hill gives views of most of the island, as well as the mainland. From Freshwater Bay, stride some 2 miles (3.2km) to the west end, where the land tapers to a point above the chalk pinnacles known as the Needles.

Wicken Fen, Cambridgeshire

The National Trust owns this nature reserve, which gives an idea of what the Fens were like before they were drained. It's a beautiful, wild wetland with paths and boardwalks, and a prize habitat for many species, including otters; trail leaflet from nature reserve.

Best places to stay

Bovey Castle Hotel (££–£££)

Luxury in the heart of Dartmoor: elegant bedrooms, ornate public rooms, a fine restaurant and championship golf course.

✉ Moretonhampstead, Devon ☎ 01647 445000; www.boveycastle.com

The Dorchester (£££)

World class; beautifully furnished bedrooms with sumptuous bathrooms – everything you would expect at this level of service.

✉ 53 Park Lane, London ☎ 020 7629 8888; www.thedorchester.com

🚇 Hyde Park Corner

The Feathers at Ludlow (££)

This historic, long-established hotel dates back to the 17th century and features exposed timbers, ornate ceilings and oak panelling.

✉ Bull Ring, Ludlow, Shropshire ☎ 01584 875261;

www.feathersatludlow.co.uk

Gravetye Manor (£££)

A stone-built Elizabethan mansion, at the end of a long drive through Forestry Commission land; the interior is characterized by highly polished wooden surfaces, open log fires, and spacious bedrooms with comfortable furniture and modern amenities.

✉ Vowles Lane, East Grinstead, West Sussex ☎ 01342 810567; www.gravetyemanor.co.uk

Manchester Marriott Victoria and Albert (££)

Imaginatively created from old warehouses, this modern hotel stands on the banks of the River Irwell and provides easy access to Manchester's heritage and shopping sites; good restaurant.

✉ Water Street, Manchester ☎ 0161 8321188; www.marriott.co.uk

Le Manoir aux Quat'Saisons (£££)

The lovely gardens around this 15th-century manor house supply the vegetables and herbs for the hotel's highly respected kitchens; an outstanding hotel and restaurant run by French chef Raymond Blanc.

✉ Church Road, Great Milton, Oxfordshire ☎ 01844 278881; www.manoir.com

The Royal York Hotel (££)

Reminiscent of an age of past elegance, this magnificently restored Victorian hotel offers a pleasing atmosphere of romantic splendour, set within its private grounds overlooking the city walls.

✉ Station Road, York ☎ 01904 653681; www.principal-hayley.com

Exploring

London	77–96
Northern England	97–116
Central England	117–140
Southeast England	141–164
Southwest England	165–186

Small as England may look on the map, it is packed with things to see and do, and the landscape and architecture can change within a few miles. Between London – one of the great capital cities of the world – and the myriad tiny villages with little more than a church and a few houses, you'll find splendid stately homes, pretty market towns, ancient monuments and fabulous gardens, as well as internationally renowned art, history, shops and festivals.

In the north are the mountains of the Lake District and the huge open spaces of Northumbria; Yorkshire and the Peak District below offer moorland and dales. In the south the coastline of the West Country contrasts with the heaths and orchards of the more populated southeast. In between are the Cotswolds, dotted with picture-perfect stone villages and the fenlands of East Anglia with their magical waterways.

London

London is one of Europe's biggest cities, with a population of over 7 million and an area spreading for more than 620sq miles (1,606sq km) from its heart along the River Thames. It is a place with unequalled charisma and an almost tangible air of constant excitement that comes as much from the amazingly cosmopolitan make-up of its resident population as from the 'buzz' of a capital city.

Yet, in spite of the constant activity, there are many oases of peace and quiet. London's public parks, gardens, museums and historic churches rival the best in the world – many of them tucked away from the traffic congestion and the brouhaha of everyday life. It's also an addictive place for shopping – whether you're splashing out in the fashion emporia, boutiques and department stores of the West End, or browsing the cheerfully ebullient weekend street markets like Brick Lane, Camden Lock or Greenwich.

✚ Q16

BRITISH MUSEUM

The British Museum, the world's first public museum, was created in 1753, following the death of Sir Hans Sloane, whose collection of over 80,000 artefacts was sold to the British government. The museum, the largest in the UK, moved to its present site in 1823 and contains over 6 million items. Worth singling out are the Elgin Marbles, the Rosetta Stone, the Oriental Collection, the Mexican Gallery and the Lindisfarne Gospels.

www.thebritishmuseum.ac.uk

✚ *London d1* ✉ Great Russell Street, Bloomsbury ☎ 020 7323 8000 🕐 Sat–Wed 10–5:30, Thu, Fri 10–8:30. Closed 1 Jan, Good Friday, 24–26 Dec 🎫 Free 🍴 Café (£); restaurant (££) Ⓜ Holborn, Tottenham Court Road, Russell Square

BUCKINGHAM PALACE

Built on the site of a brothel in 1703 to provide the Duke of Buckingham with a city residence, the palace, which was renovated during the 19th century, has served as the monarch's permanent London home since the time of Victoria. Eighteen of the 600 rooms are open to visitors for two months of the year; queues at the ticket office opposite in Green Park can be

considerable. The Changing the Guard, which takes place daily at around 11:30, from April to July and on alternate days the rest of the year, doesn't involve queuing, and is the most popular reason for visiting the palace.
www.royalcollection.org.uk

✠ *London b4* ✉ The Mall ☎ 020 7766 7300 Ⓕ Aug and Sep daily 9:45–6, last admission 3:45 ✋ Very expensive Ⓖ Green Park, Hyde Park Corner, St James's Park, Victoria

COVENT GARDEN

Taking its name from a medieval convent garden, the bustling, pedestrianized piazza of Covent Garden was laid out by Inigo Jones in 1631, and was initially a very fashionable address. Forty years later, it had developed into the main London fruit and vegetable market, and became a notorious red-light district. In the 1830s the area was cleaned up and the splendid iron and glass hall you see today was built to house the market, which it did until this moved south of the river to Vauxhall in 1974. Today only some arcading and St Paul's Church remain of the original piazza. Street musicians and entertainers are a daily sight. The Royal Opera House (➤ 96) reopened in 1999 after a major refurbishment.

✠ *London e2* 🍴 Numerous (£–££) Ⓖ Covent Garden

DOCKLANDS

Containerization brought the decline of London's enormous dockland area. For 20 years this part of the city lay derelict, until the 1980s when a development corporation was established to provide residential and office accommodation. The centrepiece is the Canary Wharf tower, at 800ft (244m), designed by Cesar Pelli. The area is connected to central London by the Docklands Light Railway (DLR), with its distinctive driverless trains and the Jubilee line, whose Canary Wharf station was designed by Sir Norman Foster.

✚ *London h2 (off map)*

GREENWICH

Steeped in royal and naval history, Greenwich (pronounced Gren-itch), boasts some of London's finest architecture in the Royal Observatory, Queen's House (a miniature palace built for the wife of James I and Britain's earliest truly classical building) and the National Maritime Museum. These are within Greenwich Park, an attractive open space in which you will also find the line and clock marking the Greenwich Meridian. Close by is the Royal Naval College.

✚ *London h3 (off map)* 🚉 DLR Cutty Sark

HYDE PARK

Hyde Park is the largest and most famous of the central London parks. If you enter at Hyde Park Corner, you pass through Constitution Arch, commemorating Wellington's victory at Waterloo. Approach from Oxford Street, and you'll pass Marble Arch, designed by Nash in 1827 to imitate the Arch of Constantine in Rome; until 1851 it stood in front of Buckingham Palace (► 78–79). Near Marble Arch is Speakers' Corner, a platform for cranks, hecklers and religious extremists, and an ideal place for a little light entertainment. The **Serpentine Gallery,** to the west of the Serpentine lake, contains contemporary art exhibitions.

✚ *London a4 (off map)* 🍴 The Lido Café (£) 🚇 Several including Marble Arch, Hyde Park Corner

Serpentine Gallery
☎ 020 7402 6075;
www.serpentinegallery.org
🕐 Daily 10–6 during exhibitions
🎟 Free 🚇 Lancaster Gate, South Kensington

LONDON EYE

Take a fun 30-minute ride on the world's largest observation wheel, erected for the millennium. On a clear day you can see 25 miles (40km) over the city. It is advisable to buy tickets in advance to avoid waiting. You can also take a London Eye River Cruise from here.

www.ba-londoneye.com

✚ *London e4* ✉ Jubilee Gardens, South Bank ☎ 0870 5000 600; 0870 990 8883 ⊙ Jun, Sep daily 10–9; Jul–Aug daily 10–9:30; Oct–May daily 10–8 ✋ Very expensive
Ⓠ Waterloo

MUSEUM OF LONDON

Beginning with a Prehistoric Gallery, then progressing chronologically, the Museum of London tells the story of the history of the capital. Very few of London's ancient buildings remain, but since World War II many important Roman, Saxon and Tudor discoveries have been made and are on display. You will also find the Lord Mayor's Coach, a replica of a Newgate prison cell and the story of the Great Fire of London.

www.museumoflondon.org.uk

✚ *London h1* ✉ London Wall
☎ 0870 444 3852 ⊙ Daily 10–5:30
✋ Free 🍴 Café (£) Ⓠ Barbican, Moorgate

NATIONAL GALLERY

Housing over 2,000 paintings, the National Gallery contains one of the finest and most comprehensive collections of Western art

in the world. The collection is divided chronologically, beginning with medieval and early Renaissance work, and includes *The Virgin of the Rocks* by Leonardo da Vinci, *Venus and Mars* by Botticelli, *Doge Leonardo Loredan* by Giovanni Bellini and *The Battle of San Romano* by Uccello. It's a good idea to stop by the Micro Gallery, where, with the aid of computers, you can plan your own tour.
www.nationalgallery.org.uk

🕇 *London d3* ✉ Trafalgar Square ☎ 020 7747 2885 🕐 Mon–Sun 10–6, Wed 10–9. Closed 24 26 Dec, 1 Jan 🍴 Free 🍴 Café (£), Brasserie (ff) 🚇 Charing Cross ❓ Tours available, and self-guided audio tours

NATURAL HISTORY MUSEUM

The museum building, constructed in neo-Gothic cathedral style in the 1870s, impresses as much as the exhibits. No visit to the museum would be complete without seeing the dinosaurs, and (unless you're squeamish about these things) the Creepy Crawlies exhibition – a great favourite with children. This is a far cry from the traditional image of a natural history museum, combining a wealth of content with imaginative new technology.

www.nhm.ac.uk

🕂 *London a4 (off map)* ✉ Cromwell Road and Exhibition Road ☎ 020 7942 5000 🕐 Daily 10–5:30. Closed 24–26 Dec 🖐 Free 🚇 South Kensington

PALACE OF WESTMINSTER

Parliament has not always met in London, but the first Palace of Westminster was built here around 1050 by Edward the Confessor, and significantly extended by William the Conqueror. There are two debating chambers, the House of Commons and the House of Lords. You can wait for a seat in the Visitors' Gallery on 'sitting days', normally Monday to Thursday afternoons (and some Fridays), by waiting outside St Stephen's entrance.

The building's best-known feature is the clock tower, Big Ben, though this is more correctly the name for its 13.4 ton bell, cast at the Whitechapel Bell Foundry in 1858 and named after Benjamin Hall, First Commissioner of Works at the time.

www.parliament.uk

✚ London d5 ✉ St Margaret Street (public entrance) ☎ Commons: 020 7219 4272; Lords: 020 7219 3107 ⏲ Tours: Aug–Sep Mon, Fri, Sat 9:15–4:30, Tue–Thu 1:15–4:30 ✋ Free ⊙ Westminster

ROYAL BOTANIC GARDENS, KEW

Containing an outstanding collection of plants, trees and flowers from all parts of the world, Kew Gardens owe their origin to Augusta, the Dowager Princess of Wales and mother of George III. In 1759, she turned part of her estate into a botanical garden, primarily for educational and scientific purposes. By 1841, however, the garden had seriously declined and was handed over to the State. The following year, Sir William Hooker was appointed director and the gardens began to acquire their worldwide reputation.

www.kew.org

✚ Q16 ✉ Kew, Richmond ☎ 020 8332 5655 ⏲ Apr–Aug Mon–Fri 9:30–6, Sat–Sun 9:30–7; Sep–Oct daily 9:30–5:30; Nov–Jan 9:30–3:45, Feb–Mar 9:30–5 ✋ Expensive 🍴 Cafés and restaurants (£–££) ⊙ Kew Gardens

ST PAUL'S CATHEDRAL

When Sir Christopher Wren completed St Paul's in 1711 it was hailed as the world's first Protestant cathedral. Work began after the Great Fire of London in 1666 had destroyed the previous cathedral. It continues to dominate the London skyline, towering above many newer buildings. Inside are Flaxman's Nelson Memorial and Steven's Duke of Wellington Monument, as well as the celebrated Whispering Gallery, with its eerie acoustic effects. Continue to the Golden Gallery for one of the finest views over the city of London.

www.stpauls.co.uk

✚ *London h2* ✉ St Paul's Churchyard ☎ 020 7236 4128 🕐 Mon–Sat 8:30–4 ✋ Expensive 🍴 The Crypt Café (£), The Refectory Restaurant (£–££) 🚇 St Paul's ❓ Tours available

SCIENCE MUSEUM

One of the world's finest collections of landmarks in industrial history, technological milestones, and truly fascinating objects, the Science Museum gives a wonderful exposition of how things work and how technology has developed. There are 40 galleries; exhibits you wouldn't want to miss include the *Apollo 10* command module,

Stephenson's *Rocket*, the prototype computer and the first iron lung. The museum is renowned for its pioneering interactive hands-on displays (there are over 2,000 of them).
www.sciencemuseum.org.uk

➕ *London a4 (off map)* ✉ Exhibition Road, South Kensington ☎ 0870 870 4868 🌐 Daily 10–6. Closed 24–26 Dec ✋ Free; charge for some individual attractions 🍴 Museum café (£), restaurant (£–££) 🚇 South Kensington

TATE BRITAIN

Tate Britain houses the national collection of British art from 1500 to the present, including the highlight, the Turner Bequest, as well as pre-Raphaelite works. Until 2000, the international modern art collection was housed here as well but these works now reside in the Tate Modern on Bankside (➤ 88).
www.tate.org.uk/britain

➕ *London d6* ✉ Millbank ☎ 020 7887 8000; recorded information 020 7887 8008 🌐 Daily 10–5:50 ✋ Free; charge for some exhibitions 🚇 Pimlico

TATE MODERN

Britain's national collection
of international modern
art from 1900 to the
present day. The most
influential artists of
the 20th century are
represented, including
Picasso, Matisse, Dalí,
Rodin, Gabo and Warhol.
www.tate.org.uk/modern

✚ *London h3* ✉ Bankside
☎ 020 7887 8888; recorded
information 020 7887 8008
🕓 Sun–Thu 10–6, Fri–Sat
10–10 🎟 Free; charge
for some exhibitions
🚇 Blackfriars, Southwark

TOWER OF LONDON

Best places to see,
➤ 50–51.

TRAFALGAR SQUARE

The heart of London, from
where all road distances
are measured, Trafalgar
Square was designed by
John Nash in the 1830s, and built in honour of Lord Nelson
following his victory at the Battle of Trafalgar in 1805. The square's
centrepiece is Nelson's Column, 187ft (57m) high, erected
between 1839 and 1842.

Close by is the **Church of St Martin-in-the-Fields,** an attractive
building, famous for its classical music concerts and its social care

unit. There is an art gallery in the crypt, and a daily clothes and crafts market is held outside in the church grounds.

✚ *London d3*

Church of St Martin-in-the-Fields

✉ Trafalgar Square ☎ Concert tickets and general information: 020 7766 1100 ✋ Free 🍴 Café-in-the-Crypt (► 93) 🚇 Charing Cross

VICTORIA AND ALBERT MUSEUM (V&A)

Originally called the South Kensington Museum, the V&A is dedicated to the applied arts, and was established to house the contents of the Great Exhibition of 1851. Today the museum displays cultural artefacts from around the world, especially from the Far East, and houses one of the world's finest collection of decorative arts. Some 8 miles (13km) and four storeys of corridors and rooms make it essential to obtain a map and index before setting off into the museum.

www.vam.ac.uk

✚ *London a4 (off map)* ✉ Cromwell Road, South Kensington ☎ 020 7942 2000 🕐 Daily 10–5:45 (Fri until 10). Closed 24–26 Dec ✋ Free 🍴 The Garden Café (£), The V&A Café (£–££) 🚇 South Kensington

WESTMINSTER ABBEY

Dating from the 13th and 16th centuries, Westminster Abbey stands on the site of a Benedictine monastery which Edward the Confessor (reigned 1042–66) sought to enlarge, close to his Palace of Westminster (▶ 85). The abbey has been the setting for the coronation of every British monarch, except Edward V and Edward VIII, since the time of William the Conqueror. Today it is still a church, in use for regular worship, and over 3,000 people, including royalty, are either buried or memorialized here. The best monuments lie beyond the choir-screen; to see these you have to pay an admission charge.

www.westminster-abbey.org

✚ *London d5* ✉ Parliament Square ☎ 020 7222 5152 🕐 Mon–Fri 9:30–3:45 and Wed 6–7, Sat 9:30–1:45. Closed Sun. (Times may vary) ✋ Expensive (free to worshippers) 🍴 Coffee stands only 🚇 Westminster, St James's Park

HOTELS

Athenaeum (£££)

This elegant hotel overlooking Green Park remains one of the most popular and friendly in London. Lovely bedrooms and a spa.

✉ 116 Piccadilly ☎ 020 7499 3464; www.athenaeumhotel.com
Ⓜ Green Park

Avonmore Hotel (££)

A privately owned, award-winning B&B with just nine bedrooms.

✉ 66 Avonmore Road, Kensington ☎ 020 7603 3121;
www.avonmorehotel.co.uk Ⓜ West Kensington

The Dorchester (£££)

See page 72.

Foreign Missions Club (£)

With only gentle emphasis on the religious atmosphere, this converted row of terrace houses offers unexpected peace and quiet and a very friendly atmosphere, at an exceptionally low price.

✉ 20–26 Aberdeen Park, Highbury ☎ 020 7226 2663;
www.thehighburycentre.org Ⓜ Highbury and Islington (10-minute walk)

Goring (£££)

The oldest privately owned luxury hotel in London, a bastion of grand service and manners, with individually designed rooms and peaceful gardens.

✉ Beeston Place, Grosvenor Gardens ☎ 020 7396 9000;
www.goringhotel.co.uk Ⓜ Green Park

Guoman Tower Hotel (£££)

A great location next to the Tower of London; large and modern.

✉ St Katharine's Way ☎ 020 7481 2575; www.guoman.com Ⓜ Tower Hill

London County Hall Travel Inn (££)

A large city-centre hotel that offers stylish, spacious and well-equipped bedrooms, and is ideal for families.

✉ Belvedere Road ☎ 0870 238 3300 Ⓜ Waterloo

Mitre House Hotel (££)

A long-established, family-run hotel with good facilities, close to Hyde Park.

✉ 178–186 Sussex Gardens ☎ 020 7723 8040 🚇 Lancaster Gate

RESTAURANTS

Alastair Little Soho (£££)

Distinctive, stylish decor and light modern European cooking are the hallmark here; reserve well in advance.

✉ 49 Frith Street, Soho ☎ 020 7734 5183 🕔 Mon–Sat 12–3, 5:30–11:30 🚇 Leicester Square, Tottenham Court Road

Anchor and Hope (££)

Excellent gastropub with a bustling, informal atmosphere, and open all day for drinks; no booking; good real ales and wines. Food is listed on a board and changes frequently.

✉ 36 The Cut ☎ 020 7928 9898 🕔 12–2:30, 6–10:30; Sun sitting at 2 only; no Mon lunchtime 🚇 Waterloo

Café-in-the-Crypt (£)

This tranquil oasis in the very heart of London lies beneath the Church of St-Martin-in-the-Fields on the edge of Trafalgar Square. Good salads, soups, sandwiches and light meals.

✉ Duncannon Street, Trafalgar Square ☎ 020 7766 1158 🕔 Mon–Tue 8–8, Wed–Sat 8am–10pm, Sun 12–6 🚇 Charing Cross, Leicester Square

Chez Gérard at the Opera Terrace (£££)

A glass conservatory on top of Covent Garden's market provides a completely different atmosphere. Great place for steak and chips.

✉ First Floor, Opera Terrace, Covent Garden Central Market ☎ 020 7379 0666 🕔 Mon–Sun 12–11:30 🚇 Covent Garden

Fountain Restaurant, Fortnum and Mason (££)

An ultra-traditionally English eating place within the best-known London food store, this is something from another era with its gilded furnishings and chandeliers. Sumptuous afternoon teas at St James's Restaurant in the same building.

✉ Fortnum and Mason, 181 Piccadilly ☎ 020 7734 8040 🕓 Mon–Sat
7:30am–11pm, Sun 12–5 🚇 Piccadilly Circus, Green Park

Gay Hussar (££)

Eastern European restaurant serving good value Hungarian food.
A favourite haunt of literary, musical and bohemian types.
✉ 2 Greek Street ☎ 020 7437 0973 🕓 Mon–Sat 12:15–2:30, 5:30–10:45
🚇 Tottenham Court Road

Gordon Ramsay (£££)

One of London's finest restaurants run by the celebrity chef.
Excellent cuisine, prepared with imagination and flair. Reservations
are essential, but are only taken up to a month in advance.
✉ 68 Royal Hospital Road ☎ 020 7352 4441 🕓 Mon–Fri 12–5, 6:30–1am
🚇 Sloane Square

Number Twelve (£–££)

See page 58.

River Café (£££)

Famous advocates of regional Italian cooking, the River Café set
new standards with familiar Italian ingredients.
✉ Thames Wharf Studios, Rainville Road ☎ 020 7386 4200 🕓 Mon–Sat
12–2:30, 7–9:15, Sun 7–9:15pm 🚇 Hammersmith

Rock and Sole Plaice (£)

This long-established 'chippie' is ideal for a late evening snack if
you're in the Covent Garden area.
✉ 47 Endell Street ☎ 020 7836 3785 🕓 Mon–Sat 11:30–11:30, Sun until
10 or 11 🚇 Covent Garden

Rules (£££)

London's oldest restaurant was opened in 1798 and was
patronized by the likes of Charles Dickens, and Edward VII and
Lillie Langtry. Serves top-quality British food.
✉ 35 Maiden Lane, Covent Garden ☎ 020 7836 5314 🕓 Daily 12–12
🚇 Covent Garden

SHOPPING

Bond Street

London's most exclusive shopping street is expensive for buying, but a great place for just looking. *Haute couture*, antiques, auction houses, fine-art galleries and jewellers predominate.

🚇 Green Park, Bond Street

Covent Garden

Head to Neal Street for speciality stores or stay in the piazza for small, individual shops in a buzzing traffic-free environment.

🚇 Covent Garden

Kensington

Inexpensive and retro clothing can be found at Kensington Market, while antiques and art abound on upmarket Kensington High Street.

🚇 High Street Kensington

Kings Road

Birthplace of the mini-skirt and the Punk movement, the Kings Road is still up-to-the-minute on street fashion.

🚇 Sloane Square

Oxford Street

London's most frenetic shopping street presents a cacophony of global styles and noise and is good for chain shops and department stores. Fashionistas should stop by Topshop's flagship store – four floors of everything right on trend.

🚇 Marble Arch, Bond Street, Oxford Circus, Tottenham Court Road

Regent Street

A handsome boulevard with many exclusive shops including gold, silver and jewellery at Mappin & Webb and Garrard & Co; toys at Hamleys; an emporium at Liberty and a huge Apple store with all the latest gadgets.

🚇 Oxford Circus, Piccadilly Circus

ENTERTAINMENT

ARTS AND CULTURE

London boasts many long-running shows, mainly in the West End, as well as mainstream theatres presenting Shakespeare and contemporary playwrights.

Barbican Centre

Europe's largest arts centre is the base for the London Symphony and English Chamber orchestras.

✉ Silk Street ☎ 020 7628 2326; www.barbican.org.uk

🚇 Barbican, Moorgate

Royal Opera House

Home of the Royal Ballet and the Royal Opera. Free lunchtime concerts and events in the Linbury Studio Theatre.

✉ Bow Street, Covent Garden ☎ 020 7304 4000; www.royaloperahouse.org

🚇 Covent Garden, Embankment

Sadler's Wells

Sadler's Wells is the centre of British contemporary dance, as well as hosting touring companies.

✉ Rosebery Avenue ☎ 020 7863 8000; www.sadlerswells.com 🚇 Angel

LIVE MUSIC AND COMEDY

The 100 Club

Originally just a jazz haunt, now soul, funk, swing and Latin sounds can be heard in this renowned subterranean club.

✉ 100 Oxford Street ☎ 020 7636 0933 🚇 Oxford Circus

Ronnie Scott's

Long-established jazz club attracting the top names.

✉ 47 Frith Street ☎ 020 7439 0947 🚇 Leicester Square

Royal Albert Hall

Famous domed building staging major concerts, including classical music. The venue for the annual Proms (promenade concerts).

✉ Kensington Gore, Knightsbridge ☎ 020 7589 8212 🚇 South Kensington

Northern England

For so long tarred (unjustly) with the dark brush of industrial grime and deprivation, the north of England has done much to clean up its image, where cleaning up was needed. But so many parts of the northern counties have always been arbours of beautiful landscape and rural retreats to rival any in England.

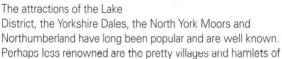

York

The attractions of the Lake District, the Yorkshire Dales, the North York Moors and Northumberland have long been popular and are well known. Perhaps less renowned are the pretty villages and hamlets of

Lancashire and Durham and the quiet backwaters of delectable Calderdale. Today bright, bustling and thriving cities – Leeds, Manchester, Liverpool and many more – play a fundamental role in the tourism and leisure industry, enabling visitors to get the best out of their stay in the North.

ALNWICK CASTLE

The 11th-century Alnwick Castle came into the Percy family in 1309, and is the birthplace of Harry Hotspur (1364–1403), who was immortalized in Shakespeare's *Henry IV Part One*. Following the revolt against Henry IV and the Battle of Shrewsbury, where Hotspur was killed, the estates were temporarily confiscated. The Duke of Northumberland still lives here, in what is the second largest inhabited castle in England. The magnificent state rooms are furnished in Italian Renaissance style.

www.alnwickcastle.com

✚ D2 ☎ 01665 511100 ⏰ Apr–Oct daily 10–5 ✋ Expensive 🍴 Café (£) and restaurant (£–££)

BERWICK-UPON-TWEED

England's most northerly town changed hands 14 times during the turbulent period when the English and Scots fought to control the borderlands. The town's 16th-century fortifications form the basis of the massively thick Elizabethan walls encircling the town, which took 11 years to complete. The town has three distinctive bridges:

the Royal Border Railway Bridge, built after the style of a Roman aqueduct by Robert Stephenson in the 1840s, contrasts remarkably with the rather modest 15-arch Berwick Bridge, completed in 1624, and the poor, concrete offering of the 1920s' Royal Tweed Bridge. By the walls, Berwick Barracks date from 1717, and museums inside include a display on the life of the British infantryman.

✚ C1 🚹 106 Marygate ✉ 01289 330733

Berwick Barracks

✉ The Parade ☎ 01289 304493: www.english-heritage.org.uk
🕓 Easter–Sep Wed–Sun 10–5 ✋ Inexpensive

CARLISLE

Carlisle is a border city, with a wide pedestrianized marketplace at its heart. Its name is derived from the Celtic word 'caer' meaning fort. Scottish and English names and accents still mingle freely in its covered market and malls, though there is little today to hint at the troubles the city has faced. It was last besieged in 1745 by Bonnie Prince Charlie's Jacobite army. Chief among the city's

assets are the castle, the striking red sandstone cathedral, and the **Tullie House Museum and Art Gallery,** which dramatically portrays much of the city's turbulent past, as a Roman frontier settlement and as a border town. Carlisle is also the terminus for the scenic Settle–Carlisle Railway.

www.historic-carlisle.org.uk

✚ B3 🚹 Old Town Hall ☎ 01228 625600

Tullie House Museum and Art Gallery

✉ Castle Street ☎ 01228 618718;
www.tulliehouse.co.uk 🕓 Nov–Mar Mon–Sat 10–4, Sun 12–4; Apr–Jun, Sep–Oct Mon–Sat 10–5, Sun 12–5; Jul–Aug Mon–Sat 10–5, Sun 11–5
✋ Moderate 🍴 The Garden Restaurant (£)

CASTLE HOWARD

The splendour of the 18th-century Castle Howard, near Malton, northeast of York, provided the setting for the television adaptation of Evelyn Waugh's *Brideshead Revisited*. There are richly furnished rooms and an outstanding estate to explore.

www.castlehoward.co.uk

✚ D5 ☎ 01653 648444 ◑ House: Mar–Oct daily 11–4. Garden and adventure playground: daily 10–6:30 (closes at dusk in winter) ✋ Expensive
🍴 Four cafés (£–££)

DURHAM

Built high on a hill within a tight meander of the wooded River Wear, Durham's compact historic centre is quite spectacular and largely traffic free. The **cathedral** is the finest example in Britain of the Norman style, all built during 1070 to 1140, and you can climb the tower and visit the treasury and former monks' dormitory. In Palace Green is the castle whose great circular keep contains the Gallery and Chapel, and the medieval Great Hall, all which are part of the university.

www.durhamtourism.co.uk

✚ D4 ✉ 2 Millennium Place ☎ 0191 384 3720 ◑ Mon–Sat 9:30–5:30, Sun and public hols 11–4

Durham Cathedral

☎ 0191 386 4266 ◑ Daily Mon–Sat 9:30–6, Sun 12:30–5:30; mid-Jul to Aug open until 8 ✋ Free (donation requested)

EDEN VALLEY

The River Eden flows down from the Pennine fells through the market towns of Kirkby Stephen and Appleby-in-Westmorland before heading for the Solway Firth. Appleby is a pretty town of sandstone buildings, notably along its main street, with Appleby Castle at the top and St Lawrence's Church at the bottom.

✚ B4

ℹ Appleby Moot Hall, Boroughgate ☎ 01768 351177

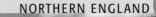

FOUNTAINS ABBEY

In 1132 13 monks, rebelling against the relaxed order of their parent house, came to Fountains to begin an austere and simple life. When the Dissolution of the Monasteries brought abbey life to an end in the 16th century, they left behind the most complete Cistercian abbey remains in Britain. Too remote to be turned into a country house, the remains evoke the spirit of the religious community that lived here for 400 years. Immediately adjacent, Studley Royal Water Garden was laid out in the 18th century with geometric ponds and follies, embellished by the abbey ruins; the garden and abbey have been designated a World Heritage Site.

www.fountainsabbey.org.uk

🟦 C5 ✉ Studley Park, Fountains, Ripon ☎ 01765 608888 🕐 Nov–Feb daily 10–4; Mar–Oct daily 10–5. Closed Fri Nov–Jan 👋 Moderate
🍴 Restaurant (£–££)

HADRIAN'S WALL

Best places to see, ➤ 42–43.

HAWORTH

On the edge of the Pennine moors, Haworth, scarcely less a literary shrine than Stratford-upon-Avon, is an attractive and busy little town famed for its cobbled streets and its association with the Brontë sisters – Charlotte, Emily and Anne, who came to live here in 1820. The Brontës were a close-knit family and their home, now the **Parsonage Museum,** formed the focus of the sisters' world from an early age. The museum displays the Brontës' own furniture and possessions, and is a good starting point for the popular Brontë Trail.

www.visithaworth.com

✚ C6 🚏 2–4 West Lane ☎ 01535 642329

Brontë Parsonage Museum

✉ Church Street ☎ 01535 642323 🕐 Apr–Oct daily 10–5:30; Oct–Mar daily 11–5. Closed 24–27 Dec and 2–31 Jan

✋ Moderate 🍴 Cafés in town (£–££)

HEBDEN BRIDGE

Although the town dates back to medieval times when it developed at the intersection of trade routes and a river crossing, it wasn't until mechanization was introduced in the 18th century that Hebden Bridge began to grow. As its textile industry flourished, the influx of workers meant that houses had to be built up the steep valley sides, giving the town its characteristic 'double-decker' housing. Some old mill buildings have been converted into museums, craft galleries and shopping areas. At the heart of the South Pennines, Calderdale is surprisingly attractive.

✚ C6
ℹ Butler's Wharf, New Road
☎ 01422 843831 🕐 Easter–Oct
Mon–Fri 9:30–5:30, Sat 10:15–5, Sun
10:30–5; Nov–Easter Mon–Fri 10–5,
Sat–Sun 10:30–4:15

HOLY ISLAND

It was on Holy Island, formerly
known as Lindisfarne, that
St Aidan of Iona founded a
monastery in the 7th century,
Lindisfarne Priory, one of the
holiest sites of Anglo-Saxon
England. This small island is only
accessible by causeway from
Beal, and only then when tides
permit. St Cuthbert lived and died
on the island, which has become
a place of pilgrimage. Lindisfarne
Castle was built in the 16th
century, to defend the harbour
from marauding Scots, and its
museum includes a collection of
inscribed stones, all that remain
of the first monastery.

✚ D1

Lindisfarne Priory and Museum
☎ 01289 389200 🕐 Apr–Sep daily
9:30–5; Oct daily 9:30–4; Nov–Jan
daily 10–2; Feb–Mar daily 10–4.
Closed 24–26 Dec and 1 Jan
✋ Moderate 🍴 Café and restaurant
in village (£)

KENDAL

The limestone-grey buildings of this busy
market town conceal a maze of yards and
'ginnels' (narrow passages). They are a
delight to explore: one contains a row of
charming almshouses, still in use. Above
the town rise the ruins of Kendal Castle,
birthplace of Katherine Parr (1512–48), the
last wife of Henry VIII. **Abbot Hall Art
Gallery,** near the church, includes works by
Ruskin, Constable and Turner. The Museum
of Lakeland Life in the adjacent stables
contains Arthur Ransome and 'Postman Pat'
memorabilia, as well as local history displays.
www.lakelandgateway.info

➕ B4 ℹ️ Town Hall, Highgate ☎ 01539 725758
🕐 Mar–Oct Mon–Sat 10–5; Nov–Feb Mon–Sat
10–4

Abbot Hall Art Gallery

☎ 01539 722464; www.abbothall.org.uk
🕐 Apr–Oct daily 10:30–5; Nov–Mar daily 10:30–4.
Closed Sun, late Dec–late Jan ✋ Moderate
🍴 The Coffee Shop (£)

LAKE DISTRICT

Best places to see, ➤ 44–45.

LANCASTER

Once an important port for the slave trade,
much of Lancaster's character comes from
the Georgian buildings of this unhappy
period, though there was much traffic in
mahogany, tobacco, rum and sugar, too.
Lancaster Castle, built around 1200 and

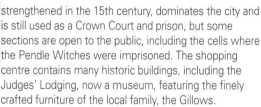

strengthened in the 15th century, dominates the city and is still used as a Crown Court and prison, but some sections are open to the public, including the cells where the Pendle Witches were imprisoned. The shopping centre contains many historic buildings, including the Judges' Lodging, now a museum, featuring the finely crafted furniture of the local family, the Gillows.

🚩 B5 🛈 29 Castle Hill ☎ 01524 32878 🕙 Apr–Nov Mon–Sat 10–5; Nov–Apr Mon–Sat 10–4

Lancaster Castle

✉ The Shire Hall ☎ 01524 64998; www.lancastercastle.com 🕙 Daily 10:30–4 ✋ Moderate 🍴 Folly Café, Castle Hill (£)

LEEDS

The largest urban development in Yorkshire and its economic capital, Leeds owes its growth, notably during the 19th century, to wool and to its position as a port on the Leeds–Liverpool and Aire and Calder canals. The area around the canals, which run through the city centre, has been developed to provide a lively waterfront culture of pavement cafés and specialist shops along the water's edge. Following large-scale urban rejuvenation, Leeds has become an outstanding nightlife destination and a major cultural centre, home to Opera North. Leeds' shopping is also a major draw; try the fashionable department store Harvey Nichols for window shopping.

www.leeds.gov.uk

🚩 C6 🛈 The Arcade, City Railway Station ☎ 0113 242 5242 🕙 Mon–Sat 9–5:30, Sun 10–4

LEVENS HALL AND TOPIARY GARDENS

This magnificent Elizabethan mansion is built around a
13th-century tower, and is the family home of the Bagots. On
display is a collection of Jacobean furniture, paintings and early
English patchwork. The award-winning topiary gardens were laid
out in 1694, and feature yews trimmed to the shape of pyramids,
peacocks and hats.

www.levenshall.co.uk

➕ B5 ☎ 01539 560321 ⏰ House: daily 12–4. Gardens: daily 10–5
✋ Expensive 🍴 Tea room (£–££)

LIVERPOOL

The city that produced the Beatles is also
renowned for its acerbic wit, a remarkable
community spirit and fiercely proud loyalty to one
of its two major football teams. Liverpool rose to
prominence through trade with the Americas,
importing sugar, spices and slaves. Its historic
waterfront is now an important tourist attraction,
centred on Albert Dock, where the warehouses
constitute one of the greatest grouping of Grade I
listed buildings in the country. They have been
converted into a complex of shops, television

studios, bars, restaurants and the Tate Gallery Liverpool, which houses an impressive collection of contemporary art. It is complemented by the **Walker Art Gallery,** with its collection of European Old Masters, pre-Raphaelite and modern British works.
www.visitliverpool.com

✚ A6 ✉ Anchor Courtyard, Albert Dock ☎ 0151 233 2008 🕓 Apr–Sep daily 10–5:30; Oct–Mar daily 10–5

Walker Art Gallery

✉ William Brown Street ☎ 0151 478 4199; www.thewalker.org.uk 🕓 Daily 10–5. Closed 24–26 Dec, 1 Jan 🖑 Free 🍴 The Walker Coffee Shop (£)

MANCHESTER

Once the world's major cotton-milling centre, Manchester, with its spruced-up Victorian buildings, extensive shopping, plentiful restaurants and enviable nightlife, is arguably one of the trendiest places in England. Manchester has undergone an urban makeover unequalled in Britain, boosted by the phenomenal success of the Manchester United football team. The area known as Castlefield, site of a Roman fort, is today the focus of Manchester's tourism industry. Many of the surrounding Victorian warehouses have been converted into apartments, hotels and tourist attractions. **Urbis** is a new kind of museum in a dramatic glass building with interactive exhibits about life in cities around the world.
www.visitmanchester.com

✚ B6 🛈 Town Hall Extension, Lloyd Street ☎ 0871 222 8223 🕓 Mon–Sat 10–5:30, Sun 10:30–4:30

Urbis

✉ Cathedral Gardens ☎ 0161 605 8200; www.urbis.org.uk 🕓 Sun–Wed 10–6, Thu–Sat 10–8 🖑 Free 🍴 The Social (£), The Modern (£–££)

NATIONAL COAL MINING MUSEUM

This award-winning museum offers guided tours underground allowing visitors to see the methods and conditions of mining from the early 1800s. There are extensive indoor and outdoor displays, a working steam winder, a train ride and pit ponies.
www.ncm.org.uk

✚ C6 ✉ Caphouse Colliery, New Road, Overton, Wakefield ☎ 01924 848806 🕑 Daily 10–5. Closed 24–26 Dec, 1 Jan 🖐 Free ❓ Under 5s not admitted on underground tour

NEWCASTLE UPON TYNE

Capital of northeast England, Newcastle has survived the decline in many of its traditional industries. The oldest part of the city is Quayside, now a fashionable oasis with restaurants, pubs and antiques shops. The 'new castle' dates from the time of William I, though the city's economic wealth grew from a regional monopoly on coal exportation introduced in Elizabethan times. The city has several galleries and theatres, including the **Laing Gallery,** which focuses on 19th-century art.
www.visitnewcastlegateshead.com

✚ D3 🛈 Central Arcade and Guildhall, Quayside ☎ 0191 277 8000 🕑 Mon–Fri 9:30–5:30, Sat 9–5:30
Laing Gallery
✉ New Bridge Street ☎ 0191 232 7734 🕑 Mon–Sat 10–5, Sun 2–5; www.twmuseums.org.uk 🖐 Free 🍴 The Café Laing (£)

NORTH OF ENGLAND OPEN AIR MUSEUM, BEAMISH

Buildings from all over the region have been reassembled at Beamish. The museum vividly illustrates life in the northeast of England in the early 1800s and 1900s, and includes a colliery village, a 19th-century manor and a north country town.
www.beamish.org.uk

✚ C3 ✉ Beamish, County Durham ☎ 0191 370 4000 🕑 Apr–Oct daily 10–5; Nov–Mar Sat–Sun, Tue–Thu 10–4 🖐 Very expensive 🍴 Several (£)

NORTH YORK MOORS

This national park in the northeastern corner of Yorkshire, easily reached from York or Whitby, has a very special character all its own. In the steep-sided green dales (valleys), you find buildings with red roofs and yellow limestone walls, beneath the largest continuous expanse of heather moorland in England. You encounter plenty of history throughout, with dramatic medieval ruins such as Rievaulx Abbey and the castles at Pickering and Helmsley, and a section of preserved Roman road known as the Wade's Causeway. Goathland and Hutton-le-Hole are classic villages with long greens.

The best walking is along the Cleveland Way. This leads around windswept escarpments, with far-ranging views from points such as Sutton Bank and Roseberry Topping. It then edges along high coastal cliffs past the spectacularly huddled fishing villages of Staithes and Robin Hood's Bay.

www.visitnorthyorkshiremoors.co.uk

✚ D4 ⓘ Castlegate, Helmsley ⓞ Mar–Oct daily 9:30–5; Nov–Feb Fri–Sun 10–4 ☎ 01439 770442

RICHMOND

It is a delight to walk around this atmospheric old town, with its medieval castle towering high above the leafy River Swale, on the edge of the Yorkshire Dales National Park. Centred on a cobbled market square with radiating wynds (narrow alleys), Richmond contains numerous Georgian buildings, including the Georgian Theatre Royal, the oldest theatre in its original form in Britain.
www.yorkshiredales.org

➕ C4

ℹ️ Friary Gardens, Victoria Road ☎ 01748 828742 🕐 Easter–Oct daily 9:30–5:30; Nov–Mar Mon–Sat 9:30–4.30 🍴 Numerous (£–£££)

SALTAIRE

Built between 1852 and 1872 by Sir Titus Salt, this village on the River Aire is a perfectly preserved vision of his industrial Utopia, modelled on buildings of the Italian Renaissance. It was originally constructed in open countryside, to provide Salt's mill workers with the benefits of fresh air, though it is now surrounded by urban sprawl. The mill, which is larger than St Paul's Cathedral in London, was once the biggest factory in the world, and was the centre of a small conglomeration of schools, hospitals, houses, parks, baths and washhouses. The **1853 Gallery** displays the world's largest collection of the works of Bradford-born artist, David Hockney.

➕ C6 ℹ️ 2 Victoria Road ☎ 01274 774993 🕐 Daily 10–6

1853 Gallery

✉️ Salts Mill, Victoria Road ☎ 01274 531163; www.saltsmill.org.uk
🕐 Mon–Fri 10–5.30, Sat–Sun 10–6. Closed 25–26 Dec ✋ Free

SIZERGH CASTLE

The ancestral home of the Strickland family for over 760 years, Sizergh Castle, near Kendal, is built around a 14th-century tower, which was extended in Elizabethan times. The castle is surrounded by attractive gardens and contains some fine examples of oak furniture and carved wooden chimney-pieces.

www.nationaltrust.org.uk

➕ B5 ☎ 01539 560951 ⏰ Castle: Easter–Nov Sun–Thu 1–4:30. Gardens: Easter–Nov Sun–Thu 11–5 ✋ Moderate 🍴 Tea room (£)

SKIPTON

At the southern edge of the Yorkshire Dales National Park (➤ 54–55), the market town of Skipton is commonly known as the 'gateway to the Dales', and traces its history back to the 7th century when it was known as Sceptone, or 'Sheeptown'. It is dominated by **Skipton Castle** at the top of the main street, which was reconstructed in the 14th century and remodelled by the

formidable Lady Anne Clifford in the 17th century. Canal trips are available on the Leeds–Liverpool Canal which passes through Skipton, a fine base for exploring the southern Dales.

www.skiptononline.co.uk

➕ C5 ℹ️ 35 Coach Street ☎ 01756 792809 🕐 Mar–Sep Mon–Sat 10–5, Sun 11–3; Oct–Feb Mon–Sat 10–4

Skipton Castle

☎ 01756 792442; www.skiptoncastle.co.uk

🕐 Mar–Oct Mon–Sat 10–6, Sun 12–6; Oct–Feb Mon–Sat 10–4, Sun 12–4 ✋ Moderate 🍴 Tea room (£)

WHITBY

The atmospheric ruins of a 13th-century abbey, a fishing harbour and quiet charm all combine to make Whitby an agreeable and fascinating place to visit. All Captain Cook's ships were built here, and the home of John Walker, to whom Cook was apprenticed, has been converted into the **Captain Cook Memorial Museum.** The abbey stands by St Mary's Church on the clifftop above the east side of the town. The church is reached by the 199 steps of the Church Stairs, which featured in Bram Stoker's *Dracula*. A Dracula Trail can be followed across the town.

www.discoveryorkshirecoast.com

➕ E4 ℹ️ Langbourne Road ☎ 01723 383636 🕐 May–Sep daily 9–5; Oct–Apr daily 9:30–4:30

Captain Cook Memorial Museum

✉ Grape Lane ☎ 01947 601900 🕐 Easter–Nov daily 9:45–5; Mar daily 11–4 ✋ Inexpensive

YORK

Best places to see, ➤ 52–53.

YORKSHIRE DALES

Best places to see, ➤ 54–55.

HOTELS

Haleys Hotel and Restaurant (££)

An elegant Victorian town house hotel just over a mile (1.6km) from Leeds city centre has one of the best restaurants in Leeds.

✉ Shire Oak Road, Headingley, Leeds ☎ 0113 278 4446; www.haleys.co.uk

Manchester Marriott Victoria and Albert (££)

See page 73.

Miller Howe (££)

An established part of the Lakeland scene with an international reputation. Many bedrooms have private balconies overlooking Lake Windermere. Dinner is a unique experience.

✉ Rayrigg Road, Windermere, Cumbria ☎ 015394 42536; www.millerhowe.com

The Royal Hotel (££)

A listed Georgian building situated at Waterloo. The hotel looks out over Liverpool Bay and has modern, well-equipped bedrooms.

✉ Marine Terrace, Waterloo, Liverpool ☎ 0151 928 2332; www.liverpool-royalhotel.co.uk

The Royal York Hotel (££)

See page 73.

Shap Wells Hotel (££)

Cumbria's largest family-owned hotel, set in secluded, wooded grounds midway between Kendal and Penrith, and only five minutes from junction 39 on the M6. An ideal base from which to explore the Lake District and Yorkshire Dales.

✉ Shap, Penrith, Cumbria ☎ 01931 716628; www.shapwells.com

Simonstone Hall Country House Hotel (££)

With lovely views over the Wensleydale countryside, this hotel is conveniently situated for exploring the Yorkshire Dales. It has a warm, friendly atmosphere and prettily decorated rooms.

✉ Simonstone, Hawes, North Yorkshire ☎ 01969 667255

White Swan (££–£££)

A civilized 16th-century coaching inn in a characterful market town on the south side of the North York Moors. Bedrooms are smart and comfortable, and there's an excellent restaurant and small bar.

✉ Market Place, Pickering, North Yorkshire ☎ 01751 472288; www.white-swan.co.uk

RESTAURANTS

Anthony's (££–£££)

See page 58.

Betty's Café Tea Rooms (£–££)

Inspired by the art deco magnificence of the *Queen Mary* liner, this supremely elegant 1930s tea room is a York institution. Excellent set teas and light meals. Also branches in Harrogate, Northallerton and Ilkley.

✉ 6–8 St Helen's Square, York ☎ 01904 659142 ⊙ Daily 9–9

The Glass House (££)

See page 58.

The Inn at Whitewell (££)

Tremendously popular and beautifully situated in the Forest of Bowland, the inn is surrounded by rolling wooded hills.

✉ Whitewell, Forest of Bowland, Lancashire ☎ 01200 448222
⊙ Daily 12–2, 7:30–9:30

Sharrow Bay (£££)

Among the top places to eat in the Lake District. Stay in the hotel if you can and let the atmosphere take over.

✉ Sharrow Bay, Howtown, Cumbria ☎ 01768 486301 ⊙ Daily lunch (from 12:30), dinner (from 7:30)

Simply Heathcote's (£££)

Sophisticated minimalist eatery serving modern British cuisine.

✉ Beetham Plaza, 25 The Strand, Liverpool ☎ 0151 236 3536 ⊙ Mon–Fri 12–2.30, 6–10, Sat 12–2:30, 6–11, Sun 12–9

Three Fishes (£–££)

Consistently interesting Lancastrian cuisine sourced from selected local suppliers in an imaginatively upgraded pub, with a good choice of wines and local beers.

✉ Great Mitton, Lancashire ☎ 01254 826888 🕓 Mon–Fri 12–2, 6–9, Sat 12–2, 5:30–9, Sun 12–8:30

ENTERTAINMENT

Bridgewater Hall

Recitals by the Hallé Orchestra and the BBC Philharmonic, plus one-off shows.

✉ Lower Mosley Street, Manchester ☎ 0161 907 9000; www.bridgewater-hall.co.uk

Everyman Theatre and Liverpool Playhouse

From Shakespeare to stand-up comedy.

✉ 13 Hope Street, Liverpool ☎ 0151 709 4776; www.everymanplayhouse.com

Grand Theatre and Opera House

Opera North and full range of theatrical productions.

✉ 46 New Briggate, Leeds ☎ 0113 222 6222; www.leedsgrandtheatre.com

Northern Stage

Modern theatre and performances by the Northern Stage Company.

✉ Barras Bridge, Newcastle ☎ 0191 230 5151; www.northernstage.co.uk

Philharmonic Hall

Concerts by the renowned Royal Liverpool Philharmonic orchestra.

✉ Hope Street, Liverpool ☎ 0151 709 3789; www.liverpoolphil.com

Royal Northern College of Music

Shows, classical music, jazz and more.

✉ 124 Oxford Road, Manchester ☎ 0161 907 5200; www.rncm.ac.uk

Central England

The densely populated central counties of England, often called collectively the Midlands, are known mostly for the large industrial centres that grew up particularly in the 19th century. Apart from such historic honeypots as Oxford, Chester, Lincoln and Stratford-upon-Avon, the Midlands has a rich industrial heritage and the big, once unfashionable cities such as Birmingham, Coventry and Stoke-on-Trent have undergone impressive revivals and now are well worth visiting.

Birmingham

You need to pick your way carefully to find the best countryside, but some of it is extremely rewarding – especially the limestone dales and high moors of the Peak District, and the western counties of Shropshire and Herefordshire. Look for magnificent stately homes, castles and gardens dotted around the region.

BIRMINGHAM

Birmingham's reputation is grim, but once you escape New Street station, Digbeth bus station or the chaotic ring roads, you'll find a city full of vitality, especially in the award-winning waterfront development in Brindley Place, built around the old canal network. The 'city of 1001 trades' was the proving ground for the founders of the Industrial Revolution – steam pioneers James Watt and Matthew Boulton, the inventor of gas lighting William Murdock, and chemist John Priestley. Again facing a huge city centre transformation, Birmingham's story can be found in the city's excellent museums and galleries, among which the state-of-the-art **National Sea Life Centre** and the **Birmingham Museum and Art Gallery** in Chamberlain Square are worth singling out.

England's second city, Birmingham today is a major jewellery manufacturing centre, and the Jewellery Quarter is a good place to explore. You can walk there from the city centre in about 15 minutes, or take a train from Moor Street.

www.visitbirmingham.com

✚ C9

🛈 The Rotunda, 150 New Street ☎ 0844 888 3883

🕓 Mon–Sat 9:30–5:30, Sun and public hols 10:30–4:30

National Sea Life Centre

✉ Brindley Place ☎ 0121 643 6777 🕓 Mon–Fri 10–4, Sat–Sun 10–5 💵 Very expensive

Birmingham Museum and Art Gallery

✉ Chamberlain Square ☎ 0121 303 2834; www.bmag.org.uk 🕓 Mon–Thu, Fri 10:30–5, Sat 10–5, Sun 12:30–5 💵 Free

BLENHEIM PALACE

The imposing 18th-century palace of Blenheim is the family seat of the Duke of Marlborough and was designed by Sir John Vanbrugh. It contains several rooms dedicated to Sir Winston Churchill, the wartime prime minister, who was born here and is buried in the church at Bladon, not far away. The nearby village of Woodstock has royal associations dating from Saxon times when the area was used as a hunting ground.

www.blenheimpalace.com

➕ P15 ✉ Woodstock, Oxfordshire ☎ 0870 060 2080
🕐 Feb–Oct daily 10:30–4:45; Nov–Dec Wed–Sun 10:30–4:45 ✋ Very expensive

BRIDGNORTH

Bridgnorth, on the River Severn, was once an important port. The old walled town (High Town) is built on a sandstone cliff and linked to the Low Town by the oldest and steepest inland funicular in

England. The old Town Hall has some stunning stained glass.

The station is now the northern terminus of the Severn Valley Railway, Britain's longest restored standard-gauge line which runs steam trains to Kidderminster.

www.visitbridgnorth.co.uk

➕ B9
ℹ️ Listley Street (in library) ☎ 01746 763257
🕐 Mon–Wed, Fri–Sat 9:30–5; Apr–Oct Thu 10–1, 2–5

BUXTON

There's a relaxing and genteel air about Buxton (named 'Aquae Arnemetiae' by the Romans), one of the highest market towns in England. It even has its own natural spring, the source of its 18th-century popularity, which you can see in the Natural Mineral Baths. You can help yourself to mineral water from St Anne's Well, next to the Pump Room, which houses an art gallery. Although the 5th Duke of Devonshire's grand design to make Buxton rival Bath and Cheltenham as a spa resort never quite made it, the plan did see the construction of some distinguished buildings, of which The Crescent, modelled on Bath's Royal Crescent, is a fine example.

Poole's Cavern, to the southwest, is worth exploring for its

stalactites and stalagmites, and a short walk from there to a 19th-century folly, Solomon's Temple, provides a fine view over the town. **www.**visitbuxton.co.uk

✚ C7 ℹ The Crescent ☎ 01298 25106 🕙 Mar–Oct daily 9:30–5; Nov–Feb 10–4

Poole's Cavern

✉ Buxton Country Park ☎ 01298 26978; www.poolescavern.co.uk 🕙 Mar–Nov daily 9:30–5:30; Dec–Feb Sat and Sun 10–4:30 👋 Moderate 🍴 Shop selling coffees and teas

CASTLETON

Dominated by the imposing ruins of Peveril Castle, the neat village of Castleton is popular both with walkers, who come to enjoy this part of the Peak District, and visitors who come to explore the subterranean world of its caverns – The Peak, Treak Cliff, Speedwell and Blue John. The ruin of **Peveril Castle,** from which the village gets its name, sits high above Cave Dale and gazes across the valley to an Iron Age fort on the imposing, but crumbling, Mam Tor.

 C7

 Castle Street  01433 620679  Mar–Nov daily 9:30–5:30; Dec–Feb daily 10–5 (times may change)

Peveril Castle

 Market Place  01433 620613  Apr, Sep–Oct daily 10–5; May–Aug daily 10–6; Nov–Mar Thu–Mon 10–4  Inexpensive

CHATSWORTH HOUSE

The home of the Dukes of Devonshire for over 400 years, Chatsworth is among the finest houses in England, and contains one of the richest collections of fine and decorative art in private hands, including works by Tintoretto and Rembrandt. The massive formal gardens are tiny in comparison to the enormous park, designed by 'Capability' Brown, which surrounds the house.

www.chatsworth.org

 C7  Bakewell  01246 565300  Late Mar to mid-Dec daily 11–4:30  Expensive  Carriage House Restaurant (£–££) and cafés

CHESTER

Encircled by medieval and Roman walls (around which there is an informative tour), the heart of Chester is the cluster of Tudor and Victorian buildings that includes the raised arcades of The Rows. This is very much a county town, and an ideal base from which to explore. The Romans built their largest fortress in Britain here, but it was much later, as trade routes with Ireland opened up, that the prosperity of the town grew. The cathedral, built between 1250 and 1540, suffers from Victorian meddling, but remains a commanding feature, worth visiting. Beyond the city walls you can cruise on the River Dee, while further afield, **Chester Zoo,** on the A41, 3 miles (5km) north of the city, is England's largest.

www.visitchester.com

➕ B7

ℹ Town Hall, Northgate Street ☎ 01244 402111 🕓 Apr–Oct Mon–Sat 9–5:30, Sun 10–5; Oct–Mar Mon–Fri 9:30–5, Sun 10–4

Chester Zoo

☎ 01244 380280; www.chesterzoo.org 🕓 Daily from 10, but closing variable throughout year ✋ Expensive

🍴 Acorn Bar, Café Tsavo and Ark Restaurant (£)

HADDON HALL

Haddon Hall is a Tudor manor house with Norman and Saxon origins, and has served as the setting for several films. During the 18th and 19th centuries the hall was virtually abandoned and fell into neglect, which proved to be a saving grace, for it evaded the attentions of the Georgian and Victorian 'improvers'. Most of what you see today dates from the 14th and 15th centuries.

www.haddonhall.co.uk

✠ C7 ✉ Bakewell, Derbyshire ☎ 01629 812855
🕐 Apr and Oct Sat–Mon 12–4; May–Sep daily 12–4
✋ Moderate 🍴 Restaurant (£)

HEREFORD

Hereford lies amid beautiful countryside and has been a cathedral city since the 8th century. Indeed it is the Norman **cathedral** which is the town's real draw. It has the world's largest chained library (with books and manuscripts from the 8th to the 15th centuries), and the Mappa Mundi, a parchment map dating from 1289, depicting the world radiating from Jerusalem.

✠ A10

Cathedral

☎ 01432 374200 🕐 Mappa Mundi exhibition: Easter–Oct Mon–Sat 10–4:30, Sun 11–3:15; Nov–Easter Mon–Sat 10–3:30. Closed Sun
✋ Cathedral: free. Exhibition: inexpensive 🍴 Cloister Café

IRONBRIDGE GORGE

Ironbridge Gorge, the crucible of the Industrial Revolution, is Britain's best centre for industrial archaeology, and today enjoys World Heritage Site status. Centred around the eponymous iron bridge, ten **museums,** which it can take a couple of days to explore, illuminate Abraham Darby's pioneering iron work and life in an industrial region. Best among these are the Blists Hill Victorian Town, the Coalbrookdale Museum of Iron, where it all started, the Coalport China Museum, and the Jackfield Tile

Museum, which houses a unique display of Victorian tiles. A 'passport ticket' allows you to visit all the sites economically.

www.ironbridge.org.uk

➕ B8

ℹ️ Ironbridge ☎ 01952 884391 🕐 Daily 10–5

Ironbridge Gorge Museums

☎ 01952 433522 🕐 Daily 10–5. Some museums closed Nov–Mar, all closed 24–25 Dec, 1 Jan ✋ Moderate–expensive

KENILWORTH CASTLE

Immortalized by writer Sir Walter Scott, Kenilworth, and the castle from which he took his inspiration, is predominantly a dormitory of Coventry, but the castle is remarkable. Begun in the 12th century, it eventually fell into the hands of John of Gaunt, who turned it into a magnificent fortified home. His son, Henry IV, used it as a royal residence, and so it remained until Elizabeth I gave it to her much favoured court advisor Robert Dudley, Earl of Leicester. These red sandstone ruins are still extensive and imposing.

➕ C9 ☎ 01926 852078; www.english-heritage.org.uk 🕐 Mar–Oct daily 10–5; Nov–Feb daily 10–4 ✋ Moderate 🍴 Tea room, Leicester's Barn (£)

LICHFIELD

The medieval market town of Lichfield, birthplace of the 18th-century writer Dr Samuel Johnson, is dominated by its distinctive three-spired cathedral which dates back over 1,000 years. The town centre has a grid of medieval streets overlaid with later, mostly 18th-century, development and makes for fascinating exploration. Seek out the Samuel Johnson Birthplace Museum on Market Square, St Mary's Heritage Centre and the museum commemorating Erasmus Darwin (grandfather of Charles) in Beacon Street.

www.visitlichfield.com

➕ C8

ℹ️ Lichfield Garrick ☎ 01543 412112 🕐 Mon–Sat 9–5

LINCOLN

The magnificent triple-towered cathedral of Lincoln dominates the landscape from every approach; it is the third largest church in Britain. The site, on a rocky hill rising from the River Witham on the northwest edge of the Fens, was first occupied by Celts, and was such an important, strategic position that the Romans built one of their four regional capitals of Britain here. Lincoln Castle was built over the original Roman town and uses some of the Roman walls. The Jew's House on Steep Hill, now a restaurant, is one of the best examples of 12th-century domestic architecture.

www.lincoln.gov.uk

🚩 E7 🖍 9 Castle Hill ☎ 01522 873800
⏰ Mon–Fri 9:30–5, Sat 10–5, Sun 11–4

LUDLOW

One of England's best-preserved medieval and Georgian towns, Ludlow is a place of endless fascination. The town's Norman castle stands in a commanding position on a hill almost surrounded by rivers. The church, St Laurence's, contains some magnificent misericords, and is a testament to the former wool-trading prosperity of the town. Timber-framed houses

and fine Georgian buildings line all the streets, and make this a delightful place to wander. History lovers take the short journey northwards to visit **Stokesay Castle,** the best-preserved 13th-century fortified manor house in England.

www.ludlow.org.uk

✚ B9 🛈 Castle Street ☎ 01584 875053 ⏲ Mon–Sat 10–5; Apr–Oct also Sun 10:30–5

Stokesay Castle

✉ South of Craven Arms off A49 ☎ 01588 672544; www.english-heritage.org.uk ⏲ Variable, see website for full details ✋ Moderate

LYME PARK

Set in a vast woodland deer park with ornamental gardens, Lyme Hall was transformed from a Tudor house into a sumptuous Italianate palace by the Venetian architect, Leoni. The park and hall were used as the setting for Pemberley in the BBC's adaptation of Jane Austen's *Pride and Prejudice*.

✚ C7 ✉ Disley, Stockport ☎ 01663 762023; 01663 766492 (recording) ⏲ Apr–Oct Fri–Tue 11–5 (hall), 8–8:30 (park); Nov–Mar 8–6 (park only) ✋ Moderate 🍴 Tea room (£)

MALVERN

Malvern is the generic name for a delightful string of towns along the base of the Malvern Hills, themselves famed for their water. The main centre is Great Malvern, dominated by its priory which has some splendid stained glass. The nearby Malvern Hills were inspiration for the great composer Edward Elgar (1857–1934), who was born not far away, near Worcester, and is buried at Little Malvern.

www.malvernhills.gov.uk/tourism

➕ B10

ℹ 21 Church Street ☎ 01684 892289 ◷ Daily 10–5 (Nov–Easter Sun 10–4)

MUCH WENLOCK

The Tudor, Jacobean and Georgian architecture in this quiet little town is perfectly reflected in the Guildhall, perched solidly on the ancient oak columns of the Butter Market. On the edge of town are the ruins of **Wenlock Priory,** an early 13th-century church.

➕ B8

Wenlock Priory

☎ 01952 727466

◷ May–Aug daily 10–5; Sep–Oct Wed–Mon 10–5; Nov–Feb Thu–Sun 10–4; Mar–Apr Wed–Sun and public hols 10–5 ✋ Inexpensive

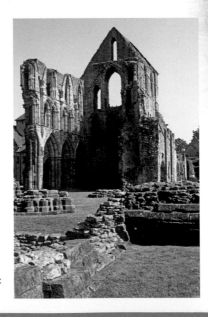

NOTTINGHAM

Built on sandstone hills at a crossing point of the River Trent, Nottingham is renowned for its association with the legendary 13th-century freebooter, Robin Hood (Sherwood Forest; ➤ 130). This is one of England's biggest cities, and is a lively, buzzing place, with a good, if changeable, nightlife, and excellent shopping. The site of the castle, demolished after the Civil War, and the old lace market are the most interesting places, along with the man-made caves, dating from medieval times, which are most easily accessible through the Broadmarsh shopping centre. Allow spare time for the Brewhouse Yard Museum on Castle Boulevard, which recreates 19th-century life. There are many claimants to be the oldest pub in Britain, but Ye Olde Trip to Jerusalem (➤ 140), hacked from the walls below the castle, has a stronger claim than most, and was in use at the time of the 13th-century crusades. D H Lawrence fans will find his birthplace museum in Eastwood, worth the 10-mile (16km) trip to see it.

www.visitnotts.com

➕ D8

ℹ 1–4 Smithy Row ☎ 08444 775678 ⏰ Mon–Fri 9–5:30, Sat 9–5, Sun 10–4

OXFORD

Best places to see, ➤ 46–47.

QUARRY BANK MILL, STYAL

A working Georgian cotton mill, built in 1784 by Samuel Greg, which provides a wonderful insight into the early years of the Industrial Revolution. The group of buildings developed around a 50-ton waterwheel, and charts the growth of cotton textile manufacture. The mill is within the Styal Country Park.

www.nationaltrust.org.uk

🔒 B7 ✉ Styal, Wilmslow ☎ 01625 527468 ⏰ Estate: daily 7–6. Apprentice House and Mill: Mar–Oct daily; Nov–Jan Wed–Sun; times vary ✋ Moderate 🍴 Mill Restaurant (£), Mill Pantry (£)

SHERWOOD FOREST

Little remains of Robin Hood's Sherwood Forest except the 450 acres (182ha) of the present country park. Extensive clearance during the 18th century makes it hard to imagine how this meagre swathe of woodland ever concealed a band of outlaws.

Just a few minutes from the visitor centre is the Major Oak, more than 30ft (10m) in diameter, where Maid Marion and Robin pledged their undying love. There may be a lot of legend about the tales of this probably fictional hero, but no one ever let that stop them having a good time.

Just north of Sherwood Forest is an area known as the Dukeries, and here you will find **Clumber Park,** a wide expanse of parkland and woods. Clumber was once the home of the Dukes of Newcastle, and though the house was demolished in 1938, many features of the estate remain, including a Gothic Revival chapel.

🔒 D7

Sherwood Forest Country Park and Visitor Centre

✉ Edwinstowe ☎ 01623 823202 ⏰ Mar–Oct daily 10–5; Nov–Feb daily 10–4

Clumber Park

☎ 01909 544917 ⏰ Park: daily during daylight hours. Gardens: Apr–Sep Mon–Fri 10–5, Sat–Sun 10–6 ✋ Pedestrians: free. Car charge: inexpensive. Gardens: inexpensive. Cycle hire: moderate 🍴 Restaurant (£)

SHREWSBURY

The River Severn determined Shrewsbury's siting, its development and its present character. The Saxon town of Scrobbesbyrig was built within a natural moat provided by a tight loop of the river, completely encircled except for a small gap – 'islanded in Severn stream', as A E Housman put it. Shrewsbury is the county town of Shropshire and claims to be the finest Tudor town in England. It's a crazy mishmash of

medieval streets, half-timbered buildings and modern shops. Among the town's most interesting buildings are the red sandstone abbey (just on the edge of town) and the Market Hall, opposite the information centre, built in 1596 for the sale of woollen cloth. But you'll find more intriguing places along

Grope Lane, Butcher Row and around St Alkmund's Church. One of the town's more famous sons is Charles Darwin. He attended Shrewsbury School, a splendid building founded by Edward VI in 1552.
www.visitshrewsbury.com
✠ B8 🛈 The Square ☎ 01743 281200 🕓 Daily 10–4; Oct–Apr closed Sun

STOKE-ON-TRENT

It is porcelain that justifies a visit to Stoke, an otherwise unattractive urban sprawl. Many of the world's most famous potteries developed here, thanks to the abundant presence of marl clay, coal, water, iron, copper and lead – the raw materials for the production of ceramics. Royal Doulton, Minton,

Spode and Wedgwood all come from here. The city itself is an amalgam of six smaller towns – Stoke, Hanley, Tunstall, Longton, Burslem and Fenton. At the Gladstone Pottery Museum in Longton, local craftspeople demonstrate the skills of producing pottery and there are exhibits at the Royal Doulton Visitor Centre in Nile Street, Burslem; the World of Spode near the train station in Church Street, Stoke; the Wedgwood Visitor Centre in Barlaston; and at the Potteries Museum in Bethesda Street, Hanley.

www.visitstoke.co.uk

✚ B7

ℹ️ Victoria Hall, Bagnall Street ☎ 01782 236000 🕐 Mon–Fri 9:15–5, Sat 10–2

STRATFORD-UPON-AVON

The birthplace of William Shakespeare, Stratford-upon-Avon is one of the busiest tourist attractions outside London. Aside from the extensive theatre complexes (➤ 140), you can visit the Bard's birthplace, a half-timbered Tudor house, now restored as a museum, and his wife Anne Hathaway's pretty cottage in the nearby village of Shottery. The town itself is dominated by Shakespeare's legacy, and guided tours, on foot and by bus, are available.

Ask at the tourist information centre for details.

www.shakespeare-country.co.uk

✚ C9 ℹ️ Bridgefoot, near bus station ☎ 0870 160 7930 🕐 Apr–Sep Mon–Sat 9–5:30, Sun 10–4; Oct–Mar Mon–Sat 9–5, Sun 10–4 ❓ Royal Shakespeare Company ☎ 01789 403444; www.rsc.org.uk

TATTON PARK

This is an exceptional example of an historic estate. The Georgian Tatton Hall sits amid a landscaped deer park with woodland walks and bicycle trails, and is most opulently decorated, providing a fine setting for the Egerton family's collections of pictures, books, china, glass, silver and furniture. Victorian grandeur extends into the gardens where you'll find Japanese and Italian themes, a rose garden and a maze.

www.tattonpark.org.uk

➕ B7 ✉ Knutsford ☎ 01625 534400
🕐 House: mid-Mar to Sep Tue–Sun 1–4.
Gardens: mid-Mar to Sep Tue–Sun 10–5; Oct to mid-Mar Tue–Sun 10–3. Park: mid-Mar to Sep Mon–Sun 10–6; Oct–Apr Tue–Sun 11–4
✋ Moderate 🍴 Restaurant (£)

WARWICK CASTLE

This striking building is often regarded as the most perfect medieval castle in England, and its sheer size is impressive. It does indeed have ancient origins, but a sizeable chunk of the castle dates from its 19th-century restoration, which turned it into a magnificent stately home. Nevertheless, it remains, a powerful and important piece of English architecture. The first building was Saxon, built in AD914 by Ethelfleda, daughter of Alfred the Great. This was followed by a wooden Norman castle, then the 14th-century stone version which remains today.

www.warwick-castle.co.uk

➕ C9 ☎ 0870 4422000 🕐 Apr–Sep daily 10–5:30; Oct–Mar daily 10–4:30
✋ Very expensive 🍴 Café and restaurant (£)

WORCESTER

Worcester, on the River Severn, first attained prominence during Roman times, when a flourishing iron smelting industry and a port were established here. Today, the city's glory is its cathedral, which has a history dating back to AD680. There are other interesting buildings around the cathedral; don't miss the 14th-century Edgar Tower, the Kings' School buildings in College Green, the Deanery, the Watergate, the Old Palace or the ruins of Guesten Hall. The Commandery building dates from the 15th century. It served as Charles II's headquarters for a time and now functions as an excellent museum devoted to the Civil War. For many, Worcester's fame rests on the manufacture here of Royal Worcester porcelain (and not forgetting Worcestershire Sauce). The porcelain factory is not far from the river.

www.visitworcester.com

✚ B9 🛈 The Guildhall, High Street ☎ 01905 726311
🕐 Mon–Sat 9:30–5

a walk around Lathkill Dale

This is a linear walk visiting one of the most delightful of the Derbyshire dales. Check the times of the buses back to Bakewell from Youlgreave before you set out.

Walk up King Street and turn into South Church Street and then left onto Yeld Road. After 100yds (90m), turn right onto a flight of stone steps and, at the top, go up a driveway and then an alleyway. At the far end, go past houses and alongside a playing field. Cross a road and go along the right-hand edge of the school grounds, then, after two fields, turn left alongside a wall to reach a valley bottom. Turn right, and soon bear left onto a lane for Over Haddon. Go through Over Haddon, turning left at the end descending to meet the River Lathkill. Turn right and walk up the valley for 2 miles (3.2km).

The first part of the dale is wooded, giving way to open, rocky scenery that typifies the contrasts of these dales.

As the dale narrows, cross a footbridge on the left and enter Cales Dale. After about 300yds (275m), cross the dale to climb steps on the other side, entering a sloping field. A well-marked route leads up to Calling Low Farm and across fields to a road. Turn left and immediately branch right, then right again behind a car park. Follow a lane down fields to a road below, and there turn left to follow the road into Youlgreave.

Take a little time to explore this lovely village before returning to Bakewell by bus (No 171, tel: 0871 200 2233). The bus stop is on the main street in Youlgreave.

Distance 6 miles (10km)
Time 3–4 hours including stops
Start point Bakewell ✚ C7
End point Youlgreave ✚ C7
Lunch The Farmyard pub, Youlgreave (£–££)

HOTELS

Edgbaston Palace Hotel (££)
Built in 1854, the Edgbaston Palace Hotel is a Grade II listed building situated 1 mile (1.6km) from Birmingham city centre.
✉ 198 Hagley Road, Edgbaston, Birmingham ☎ 0121 452 1577; www.edgbastonpalacehotel.com

The Feathers at Ludlow (££)
See page 72.

Fownes Hotel (££)
The Victorian glove factory has been converted into a successful, modern hotel with restaurant and well-furnished bedrooms.
✉ City Walls Road, Worcester ☎ 01905 613151; www.fownesgroup.co.uk/fownes

Inn at Grinshill (££)
Conveniently placed for Ironbridge and Shrewsbury, this elegant Georgian country inn has very well presented food and a good choice of wine and real ale.
✉ Grinshill, near Shrewsbury, Shropshire ☎ 01939 220410; www.theinnatgrinshill.co.uk

Le Manoir aux Quat'Saisons (£££)
See page 73.

Menzies Welcombe Hotel Spa and Golf Club (£££)
Magnificent Jacobean-style mansion set in its own parkland with extensive formal gardens and an 18-hole golf course.
✉ Warwick Road, Stratford-upon-Avon ☎ 01789 295252; www.menzies-hotels.co.uk

Old Parsonage Hotel (£££)
A handsome 17th-century former parsonage makes a comfortable city base, with antiques, open fires and a pleasant little garden.
✉ 1 Banbury Road, Oxford ☎ 01865 310210; www.oldparsonage-hotel.co.uk

Rutland Square Hotel (££)

An impressive conversion of a large red-brick warehouse, only 50yds (45m) from Nottingham Castle. The restaurant serves traditional English and French cuisine.

✉ St James Street, Nottingham ☎ 0115 941 1114; www.rutlandsquarehotel.co.uk

RESTAURANTS

Chez Jules (£–££)

This decent French restaurant in the busy centre of Birmingham has an excellent line of lunchtime specials.

✉ 5a Ethel Street, Birmingham ☎ 0121 633 4664 ⏰ Daily lunch, dinner. Closed Sun dinner in summer

Green's Café (£)

See page 58.

Grosvenor Arms (£–££)

A cheerful gastropub in an imaginatively converted Victorian building not far from Chester, with an interesting, constantly changing menu and an excellent selection of wines, malt whiskies and real ales. Spacious and inviting garden and terrace.

✉ Aldford, Cheshire ☎ 01244 620228 ⏰ Daily 12–9:30

King Charles II (££)

Although the 17th-century ambience is slightly contrived, the King Charles II nevertheless serves outstanding traditional food.

✉ 29 New Street, Worcester ☎ 01905 22449 ⏰ Mon–Sat lunch, dinner

The Oppo (££)

The best value in a food-laden street, serving imaginative international cuisine in a buzzing atmosphere. Always busy, but an ideal place to eat if you're exploring Stratford.

✉ 13 Sheep Street, Stratford-upon-Avon, Warwickshire ☎ 01789 269980 ⏰ Daily lunch, dinner

Rose and Crown (£–££)

A fine town centre inn, good for an all-day range of inexpensive bar meals and snacks.

✉ Market Place, Warwick ☎ 01926 411117 ◷ All day

Ye Olde Trip to Jerusalem (£)

Built into a rockface, this pub dates back to the 12th century.

✉ 1 Brewhouse Yard, Castle Road, Nottingham ☎ 0115 9473171
◷ Daily 11–11

ENTERTAINMENT

Hippodrome Theatre

The home of Birmingham Royal Ballet and regularly hosting the Welsh National Opera.

✉ Hurst Street, Birmingham ☎ 0844 338 5000;
www.birminghamhippodrome.com

Playhouse

With the Holywell Music Room, provides the bulk of music and theatre in Oxford.

✉ Beaumont Street, Oxford ☎ 01865 305305; www.oxfordplayhouse.com

Stratford-upon-Avon Theatres

For all things Shakespearean, the Royal Shakespeare Theatre; for contemporary works as well as Shakespeare, The Swan; and for experimental works, The Other Place (temporarily replaced by the Courtyard Theatre).

☎ 01789 403444; www.rsc.org.uk

Symphony Hall

The acclaimed City of Birmingham Symphony Orchestra performs at the acoustically magnificent Symphony Hall, which is also the venue for a host of touring productions.

✉ International Convention Centre, Centenary Square, Birmingham
☎ 0121 780 3333; www.thsh.co.uk

Southeast England

All along the south and east coasts of England, names and places ring significantly through the ages; the White Cliffs of Dover and the Seven Sisters, cliff faces defiant against the sea and continental Europe, are found here, as are villages rich in the traditions of the sea. Here you can explore quiet cobbled streets or elegant waterfronts or enjoy winding cliff-top paths.

Norwich

The southeast of England has always been the invader's route into the country and the landscape bears testimony to this in its scars and monuments. This '1066 country' embraces castles, battlefields and historic places, such as Leeds Castle in Kent, transformed by Henry VIII, or the ancient city of Canterbury, destination of Chaucer's pilgrims. The richness of the countryside unfolds before you into beautiful landscapes, earning Kent the epithet 'the Garden of England'.

BLICKLING HALL

Built in the 17th century, red-brick Blickling Hall is one of England's great Jacobean houses, famed for its spectacular long gallery, superb library and outstanding collection of furniture, pictures and tapestries. The gardens are splendid whatever the time of year, and the extensive surrounding parkland features a lake and many beautiful and relaxing walks. Concerts are held here in the summer, and cycle hire is available.

www.nationaltrust.org.uk

➕ T13 ✉ Blickling, Norfolk ☎ 01263 738030 🕐 House: Apr–Oct Wed–Sun 11–5. Park: daily dawn–dusk ✋ Moderate 🍴 Restaurant and pantry (£–££)

BODIAM CASTLE

Built in 1385, both as a defence and a home, Bodiam Castle is one of the most famous and evocative castles in Britain. The exterior is virtually complete and the ramparts rise dramatically above the moat. Enough of the interior survives to give an impression of castle life, and there are spiral staircases and battlements to explore. A small museum adds a social dimension.

www.nationaltrust.org.uk

➕ R17 ✉ Robertsbridge, East Sussex ☎ 01580 830196 🕐 Mid-Feb to Oct daily 10:30–6; Nov to mid-Feb Sat–Sun 10:30–4 (last admission 1 hour before closing) 🖐 Inexpensive 🍴 Tea room (£)

BRIGHTON

In the late 18th century the Prince of Wales, later George IV, visited Brighton and began the trend for seaside holidays. The seafront boasts elegant cream-coloured Regency terraces that extend to neighbouring Hove, but the city's most famous building is the extraordinary Indian-style Royal Pavilion. Today, Brighton has become a bohemian city with a large student population and gay community and is known for its nightlife. For a glimpse of its fishing-village roots and good shopping, head to The Lanes, a maze of narrow alleyways with interesting boutiques, antiques shops, cafés and restaurants. The

North Laine has pubs, cafés and quirky shops selling 1950s kitsch.

www.visitbrighton.com

➕ Q17

ℹ Royal Pavilion ☎ 0906 711 2255 🕐 Mon–Sat 10–5, Sun 10–4

BURY ST EDMUNDS

Bury's Norman grid street plan makes this attractive Suffolk town easy to explore. It takes its name from the 9th-century East Anglian king. Following his murder by Danish raiders, his bones were buried in the abbey and the town became a place of pilgrimage. The town, with the abbey ruins at its heart, became wealthy on the wool trade in the Middle Ages and is still a lively agricultural town today. Among its many attractive buildings are Moyse's Hall, now a local museum and the Angel Hotel which features in Charles Dickens' *Pickwick Papers*.

www.visit-suffolk.org.uk

✚ F10 ℹ 6 Angel Hill ☎ 01284 764667 ⏰ Easter–Sep Mon–Sat 9:30–5:30, Sun 10–3; Oct Mon–Sat 9–5; Nov–Easter Mon–Fri 10–4, Sat 10–1. Closed Sun, Oct–Easter

CAMBRIDGE

Cambridge, and more particularly its world-renowned university, largely developed because of the persecution experienced by students at Oxford. They arrived in the 13th century and the University's oldest college dates from this time (Peterhouse, 1284). There are 31 colleges making up the modern University, the most recent being Robinson, added in 1977. Like Oxford (➤ 46–47), the town has benefited greatly from its academic connections. It is now the home of the 'Silicon Fen' – high-tech industries growing up in the flatlands that surround the city. The centre of Cambridge is all about its glorious buildings. King's College, famed for its magnificent 15th-century chapel and superb choir, forms one side of King's Parade. A climb up the tower of Great St Mary's

Church is rewarded with a view over the whole city. The oldest colleges, built around neat courtyards, can easily be picked out. Further up a continuation of the same street stands Henry VIII's Trinity College. Between the colleges and the river lie the Backs, a series of genteel college gardens and lawns facing open fields across the water. You can hire the traditional punts to navigate the river. The biggest shopping area runs parallel to the colleges and is restrained in its modern use of the historic buildings. The Botanic Garden and the outstanding collections in the **Fitzwilliam Museum** are also worth visiting.

www.visitcambridge.org

✚ E10

🛈 Wheeler Street (moving to Peas Hill during 2009) ☎ 0871 226 8006
🕓 Oct–Mar Mon–Fri 10–5:30, Sat 10–5; Easter–Sep Mon–Fri 10–5:30, Sat 10–5, Sun 11–3

Fitzwilliam Museum

✉ Trumpington Street ☎ 01223 332900 🕓 Tue–Sat 10–5, Sun and public hols 12–5 ✋ Free

CANTERBURY

Canterbury was a capital as long ago as the Iron Age, and a major Roman town. In AD597, St Augustine founded the monastery, Christ Church, which became the first cathedral in England. Its magnificent Gothic successor, largely dating from the 12th century, is Canterbury's greatest treasure. The archbishop Thomas Becket was brutally murdered here in 1170, and his shrine became one of the most popular in Europe, second only to Rome – a pilgrimage immortalized by Chaucer in *The Canterbury Tales* (1388). Today the Archbishop of Canterbury is head of the Church of England and leader of the worldwide Anglican community.

www.canterbury.co.uk

✚ S16

🛈 12/13 Sun Street, The Buttermarket ☎ 01227 378100 🕓 Easter–Oct Mon–Sat 9:30–5 (until 6 Jul–Aug), Sun 10–4; Nov–Mar Mon–Sat 9:30–5

CHARTWELL

The home of Sir Winston Churchill from 1924 until the end of his life, Chartwell is an unpretentious Victorian country house, with stunning views over the Weald (► 157), and it became the place from which he drew inspiration. The rooms remain much as he left them, with pictures, maps and personal mementoes that strongly evoke the career and wide-ranging interests of England's wartime prime minister. The beautiful terraced gardens contain his garden studio in which many of his paintings are displayed.

✚ R16 ✉ Westerham, Kent ☎ 01732 868381; 01732 866368 (recorded information) ⚇ Apr–Jun Wed–Sun 11–5; Jul–Aug Tue–Sun 11–5; Sep–Oct Wed–Sun 11–5 ✋ Expensive 🍴 Restaurant (£–££)

THE CHILTERNS

The Chilterns are a range of chalk hills extending in a curve from Dunstable in the north to Reading in the south, characterized by their beech woodlands and pretty villages. Fingest is the prettiest of these, nestling in wooded downland with a Norman church and 18th-century inn. The area has been well protected from the advances of London's suburbia, but remains extremely accessible from the capital, with fast train and

tube links delivering you to the heart of this surprisingly quiet countryside. The western edge is marked by a chalkland ridge, traversed by the Ridgeway National Trail, itself following a prehistoric trade route, making excellent walking territory.

www.chilternsaonb.org

P15

Paul's Row, High Wycombe 01494 421892 Mon–Thu 9:30–5, Fri 9:30–4:30, Sat 9:30–4

DOVER CASTLE

Dover Castle is a formidable defensive structure, and was used as such from the 12th century until the 1980s. Overlooking the town, it has a massive keep built by Henry II in the 1180s, with walls 17–22ft (5–7m) thick. During the Civil War, the castle was seized by Oliver Cromwell. It was further strengthened during the Napoleonic Wars and played an important role in World War II. Dover's famous White Cliffs are honeycombed with fortifications used during this conflict. Admiralty Lookout in the castle grounds is a great place for views of the cliffs and across the Channel. The proximity to German guns on the French coast earned the defences the title 'Hellfire Corner'. In the town centre, the **Dover Museum** tells the story of the development of the town and port, and includes the Dover Bronze Age Boat which is displayed in a gallery with information on the Bronze Age.

www.english-heritage.org.uk

S17 01304 211067 Apr–Jul and Sep daily 10–6; Aug daily 9:30–6; Oct daily 10–5; Nov–Jan Thu–Mon 10–4; Feb–Mar daily 10–4 The Keep Restaurant (£) and The Tunnel Café (£) Expensive

Dover Museum

Market Square, Dover 01304 201066; www.dover.gov.uk/museum

Mon–Sat 10–5:30, Sun 12–5 Inexpensive

ELY

Until the surrounding fens were drained, in the 17th century, the Isle of Ely was indeed an island, in the middle of a labyrinth of water-filled channels and overhanging foliage. So formidable a natural defence were the marshes, that those opposing the Norman invasion were able to do so until 1071. To mark their ultimate victory, the Normans built the massive 'Cathedral of the Fens', which towers above the low-lying land. Ely is an agreeable jumble of time-warped buildings dating from the 15th century to Georgian and Victorian times.

✚ E9

ℹ Oliver Cromwell's House, 29 St Mary's Street ☎ 01353 662062

🕐 Apr–Oct daily 10–5:15; Nov–Mar Sun–Fri 11–4, Sat 10–5

HASTINGS

Hastings gives its name to the most celebrated battle in history, when in 1066 William of Normandy's conquest of England began. By the time he landed nearby, Hastings was already a flourishing port. Today, it is a pleasing mixture of contemporary seaside resort, artists' retreat and a small fishing port. Look for the tall weather-boarded fishing-net stores, unique to the town. The site of the battle is nearby at Battle, where you can tour the battlefield;

as an act of contrition for killing the English king, William built the magnificent abbey here.
www.visithastings.com

✚ R17

🛈 Queen's Square, Priory Meadow ☎ 0845 274 1001 🕓 Mon–Fri 8:30–6:15, Sat 9–5, Sun 10:30–4:30

HEVER CASTLE

The childhood home of Anne Boleyn, second wife of Henry VIII, and where Anne of Cleves, his fourth wife, lived after their divorce, Hever Castle is a fine, moated stronghold and contains many Tudor artefacts, paintings and other interesting objects. Having fallen into disrepair, the 13th-century castle was bought by William Waldorf Astor, the American millionaire owner of *The Observer* newspaper, who had it restored, and, though the Astor family no longer owns it, the castle remains a splendid example of regal life in Tudor times.
www.hevercastle.co.uk

✚ R16 ✉ Hever, near Edenbridge, Kent ☎ 01732 865224 🕓 Castle. Mar–Easter Wed–Sun 12–4; Easter–Oct daily 12–5; Nov Thu–Sun 12–3. Gardens: Mar–Easter Wed–Sun 10:45–4; Easter–Oct daily 10:45–5; Nov Thu–Sun 10:45–3. Closed Dec–Feb 💷 Expensive 🍴 The Moat and the Pavilion restaurants (£)

LEEDS CASTLE

Originally a Saxon royal manor built in AD857, Leeds Castle, which in its present form was begun in 1120, became the home of the Norman Crevecoeur family and later a royal palace during the reign of Edward I. The castle, which rises fairy tale-like from a lake, has been the home of six medieval queens, and is a delightful place to visit. If you're travelling out from London Victoria, buy an all-inclusive rail ticket to Bearsted, which includes coach shuttle and entry to the castle. www.leeds-castle.com

➕ R16 ✉ Leeds, near Maidstone, Kent ☎ 01622 765400 🕒 Apr–Sep daily 10:30–5:30; Oct–Mar daily 10:30–3:30 ✋ Expensive 🍴 The Fairfax Restaurant and Café Bar (£–££)

LULLINGSTONE ROMAN VILLA

The villa was only discovered in 1939, and ranks as one of the major archaeological finds of the 20th century. It was built around AD100, and was in use throughout the Roman occupation. Much of the villa's layout is visible, as are a number of mosaic floors.

➕ R16 ✉ Lullingstone Lane, Eynsford, Dartford, Kent ☎ 01322 863467 🕒 Apr–Sep daily 10–6; Oct–Nov and Feb–Mar daily 10–4; Dec–Jan Wed–Sun 10–4 🍴 Eynsford village ✋ Moderate

NORFOLK BROADS

Flowing through the heart of Norfolk is a spread of waterways known as 'The Broads', an area of slow-flowing rivers – the Yare,

Waveney, Bure, Ant and Thurne – and shallow lakes, 42 in all, that were created by the extraction of peat, and subsequent flooding, several hundred years ago. Sailing and cruising on the Broads are popular pursuits, and the wildlife on the Broads is second to none. The only efficient way of exploring the Broads is, of course, by boat, and you could easily spend many days here meandering around over 130 miles (210km) of lock-free, navigable waterways.
www.broads-authority.gov.uk

🔀 T13

ℹ️ Station Road, Hoveton ☎ 01603 782281 🕐 Easter–Oct daily 9–5

NORWICH

Whatever your interests, the market city of
Norwich has something to offer: architecture, art,
museums, leisure activities or simply shopping.
The slender-spired cathedral, surrounded by
cobbled streets with fine old buildings, and the
bustling, modern shopping centres are all
dominated by a Norman castle, built around 1160,
which itself houses a fine museum. Norwich is
particularly well endowed with medieval churches
(though not all are still in use), notably St John
Maddermarket, which contains a fine collection of
monumental brasses and St Michael at Plea,
which takes its name from the archdeacon's court.
Undoubtedly a wealthy medieval city, Norwich is
still East Anglia's unofficial capital, and a useful
base from which to explore the Broads and the
beautiful Norfolk coastline.

www.visitnorwich.co.uk

✚ T13

🛈 The Forum, Millennium Plain ☎ 01603 727927 ◴ Apr–Oct Mon–Sat
9:30–6, Sun 10:30–4:30; Nov–Mar Mon–Sat 9:30–5:30

PENSHURST PLACE

The delightful village of Penshurst lies at the confluence of the
rivers Eden and Medway and is dominated by 14th-century
Penshurst Place. The finest privately owned manor house in Kent,

it was the birthplace of Sir Philip Sidney (1554–86), the English poet and Elizabethan soldier. The massive chestnut roof of the Barons Hall in Penshurst Place, built by Sir John de Pulteney, four times Mayor of London, is its most spectacular feature. The house is set in magnificent formal gardens.

www.penshurstplace.com

🕂 R16 ✉ Penshurst, near Tonbridge, Kent ☎ 01892 870307 ⓘ House: Mar–Oct daily 12–4. Grounds: Apr–Nov daily 10:30–6 ✋ Moderate 🍴 Garden Tea Room (£)

RYE

Easily reached by train from London, this perfectly preserved little medieval hill town was originally a port, but the sea has receded. Mermaid Street, with its cobblestones and half-timbered Mermaid Inn is particularly photogenic, but a stroll around reveals many more gems, including the defensive gateway called Landgate, the ancient Ypres Tower with its adjacent Gun Garden sporting five cannons, and the old houses around the church. The town model in the heritage centre vividly sets the scene. Rye has plenty of antiques and crafts shops, and nearby Winchelsea is another enchanting former port, laid out on a grid in the 13th century.

🕂 R17

ℹ Strand Quay ☎ 01797 226696 ⓘ Mar–Oct Mon–Sat 9:30–5; Nov–Feb 10–4

SAFFRON WALDEN

This old market town's numerous timber-framed houses are a particular delight, many adorned with fine examples of the decorative plasterwork known as pargeting. There is a maze of medieval alleyways around the marketplace, and book and antiques shops along Church Street. Until the 18th century, this was the main centre for growing the saffron crocus, and the wealth from the trade helped build the magnificent church of St Mary the Virgin. The town has a gate into the grounds of Audley End House (► 64).

➕ E10 🚹 1 Market Place, Market Square ☎ 01799 524002 🕓 Apr–Oct, Mon–Sat 9:30–5:30; Nov–Mar Mon–Sat 9:30–5

ST ALBANS

According to tradition, Alban was a Roman soldier who converted to Christianity, and was tortured and beheaded because of his refusal to sacrifice to pagan gods. He became England's first Christian martyr, and the abbey, founded here by King Offa of Mercia in the 8th century on the site of his martyrdom, rose to be one of the wealthiest in the country. Its massive stone gateway still stands to the west of the cathedral.

St Alban's today is a thriving shopping and business centre, but it has always held an important position as a staging post on the highway to London from the north, and remains popular with

visitors. South of the town, the **Gardens of the Rose,** with over 30,000 specimens, is the world's largest rose collection.
www.stalbans.gov.uk

✚ Q15 🛈 Town Hall, Market Place ☎ 01727 864511 🕓 Mon–Sat 10–5, Sun (during school hols) 10–4

Gardens of the Rose

☎ 01727 850461 🕓 Jun–Sep Wed–Sun 11–5 💲 Moderate

SEVEN SISTERS

The country park that includes this famous landmark has some of the finest coastal and riverside walking in the country, notably along the serpentine River Cuckmere down to which the western end of the Seven Sisters dips. The Seven Sisters themselves are a stunning switchback of vertical chalk cliffs between Cuckmere Haven and Birling Gap.
www.sevensisters.org.uk

✚ R17 🛈 Seven Sisters Country Park, Exceat, Seaford, East Sussex ☎ 01323 870280 🕓 Easter–Oct daily 10:30–4:30; Nov–Easter weekends only 11–4

SUFFOLK COAST AND HEATHS

From its gently curving beaches to expansive wild heaths, reedbeds and wide estuaries, the Suffolk Coast and Heaths Area of Outstanding Natural Beauty is a striking but fragile landscape. It extends roughly from Kessingland in the north to Aldeburgh. The coast is especially treasured for its wealth of wildlife and there is a splendid marshland bird reserve at Minsmere between Southwold and Leiston. Southwold itself, genteel and upmarket, is full of old-fashioned nautical charm with its lighthouse, colourful beach huts and evocatively unchanged Sailors' Reading Room.

www.suffolkcoastandheaths.org

✚ T14

ℹ 69–69a High Street, Southwold

☎ 01502 724729 🕙 Apr–Oct Mon–Fri 10–5, Sat 10–5:30, Sun 11–4; Nov–Mar Mon, Tue, Thu, Fri 10:30–3:30, Wed 10:30–3, Sat 10–4:30

WALMER CASTLE

Intended to withstand the assaults of the French and Spanish following Henry VIII's break with the Roman Catholic Church, Walmer Castle has an original design (gunpowder had suddenly become a new threat) that is low and squat with massively thick walls. Later the castle was transformed into a stately home and became used as the residence of the Lord Warden of the Cinque Ports; the former Lord Wardens include Pitt the Younger, the Duke of Wellington and Sir Winston Churchill.

🔲 S16 ✉ Kingsdown Road, Walmer, Kent ☎ 01304 364288 🕐 Apr–Sep daily 10 6; Mar and Oct Wed–Sun 10–4 ✋ Moderate 🍴 Tea room (£)

THE WEALD

A varied and fascinating landscape between the chalkland scenery of the North and South Downs. Its name comes from the Old English word for woodland; the whole area was densely forested during Anglo-Saxon times. It became important for iron production before the Industrial Revolution. The **open-air museum** at Singleton is England's leading museum of historic buildings and traditional rural life.

www.highweald.org

🔲 R17

Weald and Downland Open Air Museum

✉ Singleton, near Chichester

☎ 01243 811363;

www.wealddown.co.uk 🕐 Jan–Feb Wed, Sat, Sun 10:30–3; Mar daily 10:30–3; Apr–Oct daily 10:30–5; Nov to mid-Dec daily 10:30–3 ✋ Moderate

WINDSOR

The handsome market town of Windsor boasts the largest castle in England, within the bounds of which is something approaching another small, walled town. The attractive streets, many of them cobbled, have numerous Georgian and timber-framed houses and an outstanding Guildhall, designed by Sir Christopher Wren. The town is, of course, dominated by **Windsor Castle,** which is still occupied by the Queen. Work started on the castle in the 11th century, though most of the buildings are 12th century and were altered in the 19th century and in the 20th following a disastrous fire in 1992. Highlights include St George's Chapel, with its fan vaulting, and the wonderfully detailed Queen Mary's Dolls' House. Across the Thames is the exclusive Eton School.

www.windsor.gov.uk

➕ Q16

ℹ️ Windsor Royal Station ☎ 01753 743900 🕐 Mon–Sat 10–5, Sun 11–4

Windsor Castle

☎ 020 7766 7304; www.royalcollection.org.uk 🕐 Mar–Oct daily 9:45–4; Nov–Feb daily 9:45–3 💷 Expensive

WOBURN ABBEY

The palatial 18th-century mansion of Woburn Abbey contains a fine private collection of art including pieces by Van Dyck, Canaletto, Gainsborough, Rembrandt and Velázquez, as well as some exquisite porcelain. A large part of the parkland forms the **Woburn Safari Park,** the largest drive-through reserve in Britain.

www.woburnabbey.co.uk

➕ D10 ✉️ Woburn ☎ 01525 290666 🕐 Mid-Mar to late Sep daily 11–4; deer park daily all year 10–5 💷 Expensive 🍴 Duchess Tearoom (£)

Woburn Safari Park

☎ 01525 290407; www.woburnsafari.co.uk 🕐 Mar–Oct daily 10–5; Nov–Dec Sat–Sun 10–3 💷 Moderate–very expensive (according to season)

a drive around the South Downs

Leave Chichester by heading north on the A286 for Midhurst, but just after Mid Lavant turn onto the B2141, following a delightful route through wooded downland to Chilgrove and South Harting.

Chilgrove is little more than a handful of cottages and a pub in a richly green valley, dotted with isolated farms; there are the remains of two Roman villas near by.

Just as the B-road leaves South Harting, turn right onto a minor road to East Harting, Elsted and Lower Elsted and,

ultimately, meet the A272 at Stedham Common. Turn right and shortly left for the hamlet of Iping, where you cross the River Rother.

Iping is an attractive Downs village of old cottages, a mill and a five-arched bridge spanning the river. Stedham Common is scattered with prehistoric burial mounds.

A short way further on, turn right and follow country lanes towards Easebourne. When you meet the A286, turn right and go into Midhurst.

Midhurst is a busy market town with a wide, spacious

North Street that contains many attractive buildings, including the substantial remains of Cowdray Castle, a Tudor mansion destroyed by fire in 1793 and retained as a romantic ruin.

In the centre of Midhurst, where the road makes a pronounced bend, look for the turning, on the right, to Bepton and follow this to a T-junction, near the hamlet. Turn left to Cocking, a roadside village in a wooded gap. Continue to follow the A286 to West Dean, a lovely place with lots of flint cottages. From West Dean, stay on the main road to return to Chichester.

Distance 55 miles (88km)
Time 2–3 hours plus stops
Start/end point Chichester ✚ P17
Lunch There are country pubs in Chilgrove, South Harting, Elsted, Lower Elsted, Easebourne, Midhurst, Cocking and West Dean

HOTELS

Beauport Park Hotel (££)
A Georgian country house set in parkland with its own swimming pool, tennis courts, putting green, candle-lit restaurant and open log fires; close to 18- and 9-hole golf courses.
✉ Battle Road, Hastings, East Sussex ☎ 01424 851222;
www.bannatyne.co.uk/hotel-hastings

Drakes (££–£££)
This hip boutique hotel on the seafront has 20 rooms and is best for those wanting to explore Brighton's lively nightlife.
✉ 43–44 Marine Parade, Brighton ☎ 01273 696934;
www.drakesofbrighton.com

Gravetye Manor (£££)
See pages 72–73.

Hotel du Vin (££–£££)
Right in the heart of historic Cambridge, this has 41 stylish rooms. You can eat well in the bistro or enjoy a leisurely afternoon tea.
✉ Trumpington Street, Cambridge ☎ 01223 227330; www.hotelduvin.com

Jeakes House (££)
A character-laden and thoroughly civilized little retreat in the historic centre of Rye, with individually furnished rooms.
✉ Mermaid Street, Rye, East Sussex ☎ 01797 222828;
www.jeakeshouse.com

The Norfolk Mead Hotel (££)
Near Norwich and the Norfolk Broads, the hotel stands in secluded grounds by the River Bure, and has an excellent restaurant.
✉ Church Loke, Coltishall, near Norwich, Norfolk ☎ 01603 737531;
www.norfolkmead.co.uk

Ravenwood Hall Hotel (££)
Set in 7 acres (3ha) of woodland and landscaped gardens just outside Bury St Edmunds, this is a hotel of character and quality.

All the bedrooms are spaciously designed and thoughtfully equipped, and the welcoming restaurant provides a fixed-price menu. Outdoor heated pool.

✉ Rougham, Bury St Edmunds, Suffolk ☎ 01359 270345; www.ravenwoodhall.co.uk

RESTAURANTS

Augustine's (££)
Popular restaurant right in the centre of town serving modern European cuisine.

✉ 1 and 2 Longport, Canterbury, Kent ☎ 01227 453063 🕐 Daily 12–2, 6–9:30

The Crooked Barn (££–£££)
Described as Oulton Broad's hidden oasis, this 18th-century thatched barn is a magnificent place to dine. The style of cuisine is 'New World' with excellent set menu lunches.

✉ Ivy House Farm Hotel, Ivy Lane, Oulton Broad, Lowestoft, Suffolk ☎ 01502 501353 🕐 Daily 12–1:45, 7–9:30

The Jolly Sportsman (£–££)
See page 58.

The Old Fire Engine House (££)
Owned and run by the same family for 30 years, this is an 18th-century building with a large walled garden and informal atmosphere. The cooking is based on local ingredients.

✉ 25 St Mary's Street, Ely, Cambridgeshire ☎ 01353 662582 🕐 Mon–Sat lunch, dinner, Sun lunch and teas. Closed for two weeks over Christmas

The Orangery (£££)
Modern English cooking served with skill in a delightful Georgian setting. Eating here gives a distinct feeling of being in a typical country home.

✉ Congham Hall Country House Hotel, Grimston, near King's Lynn, Norfolk ☎ 01485 600250 🕐 Daily 12–1:45, 7–9:15

Terre à Terre (££–£££)

Exciting vegetarian restaurant in the centre of Brighton with organic wine and beer also on the menu.

✉ 71 East Street, Brighton ☎ 01273 729051 🕐 Tue–Fri 12–10:30, Sat 12–11, Sun 12–10

ENTERTAINMENT

Arts Theatre

Cambridge's main theatre, which launched the careers of actors such as Stephen Fry and Derek Jacobi, provides an eclectic range of productions.

✉ 6 St Edward's Passage, Cambridge ☎ 01223 503333; www.cambridgeartstheatre.com

Bournemouth International Centre

Three venues in one in this popular resort town.

✉ Exeter Road, Bournemouth ☎ 08701 113000; www.bic.co.uk

Chichester Festival Theatre

Classic and contemporary theatre.

✉ Oaklands Park, Chichester, West Sussex ☎ 01243 781312; www.cft.org.uk

Komedia

Alternative theatre and stand-up comedy.

✉ 44–47 Gardner Street, Brighton ☎ 01273 647100; www.komedia.co.uk

Norwich Arts Centre

One of East Anglia's top venues for the performing arts. A varied programme of comedy, art, dance, theatre and music from international names and new talent.

✉ Reeves Yard, off St Benedict's Street, Norwich ☎ 01603 660352; www.norwichartscentre.co.uk

Southwest England

Bristol

The southwest, also known as the West Country, reaches from Gloucester on the River Severn all the way to Land's End, and has some of the most naturally beautiful tracts of countryside anywhere in England. Here leafy lanes and flowering hedgerows pattern rolling green hills and link picture-

postcard villages with thatched cottages, stately homes, riverside pubs and prehistoric sites that tell so much of England's heritage.

Two great national parks, Dartmoor and Exmoor, provide wide, open spaces and the chance to escape and unwind, and these are supplemented by a string of Areas of Outstanding Natural Beauty and England's newest national park in the New Forest. Above all, the southwest is a land of rich pastures that produce some of England's finest meat, cheeses and milk; it is also a top cider-producing area, able to boast cider of national and international reputation.

AVEBURY

The village of Avebury stands largely within a stone circle that rivals Stonehenge though the individual stones are smaller. An enormous earthwork encloses the main circle, which is thought to have been built around 2500BC. On first impressions it is difficult to grasp what this UNESCO World Heritage Site is about, but this is partially rectified by the **Alexander Keiller Museum** at the west entrance.

➕ N16 ⊗ Stone circle: daily

Alexander Keiller Museum

☎ 01672 539250 ⊗ Apr–Oct daily 10–6; Nov–Mar daily 10–4 🍴 In village (£) 🎫 Inexpensive

BATH

Best places to see, ➤ 36–37.

BRISTOL

Bristol ensured its place as an inland port to rival London from the Middle Ages, when its wealth grew on the trade in slaves, cocoa, sugar, tobacco and manufactured goods between the New World and Africa. Many of the buildings from this period were damaged during World War II, though some remain intact.

In the 19th century, the engineer Brunel created two of the city's

most famous monuments, the SS *Great Britain,* the world's first ocean-going steamship with screw propulsion, and the spectacular

Clifton Suspension Bridge, a magnificent structure high above the Avon Gorge. The docks have been redeveloped and now offer eateries, family attractions and museums.

www.visitbristol.co.uk

✚ M15

ℹ️ Explore at Bristol, Anchor Road ☎ 0906 7112191

🕓 Daily 10–5

BUCKLAND ABBEY

Concealed in a secluded valley above the River Tavy, Buckland used to be a small but prominent Cistercian monastery. The house incorporates the ruins of the 13th-century abbey church, and has strong connections with the explorer Sir Francis Drake and his rival, Sir Richard Grenville.

www.nationaltrust.org.uk

✚ J17 ✉ Yelverton ☎ 01822 853607 🕓 Feb to mid-Mar Sat, Sun 2–4:15; mid-Mar to Oct Fri–Wed 10:30–4:45; Nov–Dec Fri–Sun 12–3:15 ✋ Moderate
🍴 Restaurant and tea room (£)

CHEDDAR GORGE

Slicing through the Mendip Hills, this limestone gorge is an impressive and beautiful natural phenomenon. The road through the gorge runs for about 2 miles (3.2km) and, at its narrowest, passes below cliffs almost 500ft (152m) high. Beneath the gorge the **Cheddar Caves** were fashioned by subterranean rivers during the last Ice Age, and were later occupied by prehistoric people.

🚻 L16 🛈 The Gorge, Cheddar
☎ 01934 744071 🕓 Daily 10–5

Cheddar Caves

☎ 01934 742343; www.cheddarcaves.co.uk
🕓 Jul–Aug daily 10–5:30; Sep–Jun daily 10:30–5
✋ Expensive 🍴 Café (£)

CHELTENHAM

The spa town of Cheltenham, well known for its racecourse and its ladies' college, is an excellent place from which to explore the Cotswolds. Most visitors come here now for the architecture rather than the waters. The town suffers from unimaginative planning that sprinkles shopping centres in among attractive squares, gardens and elegant, Regency-period buildings. Ironically, the civic offices are one of the best features of Cheltenham, and a delightful thoroughfare. The **Pittville Pump Room,** a mile (1.6km) from the town centre, in an area of villas and parkland, is one of the town's finest examples of the Regency style, constructed as a spa and social centre for Joseph Pitt's new estate. The **Art Gallery and Museum** has sections covering William Morris, the English craftsman, poet and socialist, and the Arts and Crafts Movement, which sprang from his association with pre-Raphaelite colleagues. Lovers of classical music will want to visit No 4 Clarence Road where composer Gustav Holst, best known for *The Planets,* was born. Displays include Holst memorabilia and descriptions of life in the 19th and early 20th century.

www.visitcheltenham.com

✚ B10 🚹 The Promenade ☎ 01242 522878 🕓 Mon–Sat 9:30–5:15

Pittville Pump Room

✉ Pittville Park ☎ 01242 523852 ✋ Free

Art Gallery and Museum

✉ Clarence Street ☎ 01242 237431; www.cheltenhammuseum.org.uk
🕓 Apr–Oct daily 10–5; Nov–Mar daily 10–4 ✋ Free

COTEHELE HOUSE

Leaning into the hillside above the River Tamar, Cotehele was mainly built between 1485 and 1627, and was, for centuries, the home of the Edgcumbe family. This is a small and fragile house; consequently no more than 80 visitors are allowed inside at any one time, so be prepared to wait for entry. The house contains tapestries and original furniture and armour, but if you have to wait, the formal gardens, which overlook a valley garden, will agreeably pass your time.

✚ J17 ✉ St Dominick, near Saltash ☎ 01579 351346; information line: 01579 352739 🕓 House: mid-Mar to Oct Sat–Thu 11–4. Garden: daily 10–dusk ✋ Moderate 🍴 Restaurant and tea room (£)

THE COTSWOLDS

Best places to see, ➤ 38–39.

DARTMOOR

Wild, bleak, high and windswept, Dartmoor is the only true wilderness in southern England. It occupies the main part of the country between Exeter and Plymouth, and has a 'grim charm', alluded to by Sir Arthur Conan Doyle in *The Hound of the Baskervilles*. But it has a distinct beauty too, that should compel everyone to cross its barren moors at least once. That prehistoric people found it less forbidding is evidenced by the scattered remnants of mostly Bronze and Iron Age presence. The remains of tin and copper mining are also to be found here and the museum at **Morwellham Quay** is a fascinating place to learn about this aspect of the region's history. Dartmoor has been a protected **national park** since 1951.

➕ K17

Morwellham Quay

✉ Morwellham ☎ 01822 832766; www.morwellham-quay.co.uk
🕓 Easter–Oct daily 10–5; Nov–Easter daily 10–4 💷 Free

Dartmoor National Park

ℹ High Moorland Visitor Centre, Tavistock Road, Princetown ☎ 01822 890414; www.dartmoor-npa.gov.uk 🕓 Daily 10–5 (winter daily 10–4)

DORCHESTER

For lovers of Thomas Hardy's works, this is the place to visit – he was born just 3 miles (4.8km) away at Higher Bockhampton. Hardy worked as an architect in the town, and his novel, *The Mayor of Casterbridge*, describes the town as it was in the mid-19th century. The High Street is particularly handsome, and boasts a variety of Georgian town houses. The 18th-century Shire Hall contains the old county court, preserved as a memorial to the Tolpuddle Martyrs who were tried here in 1834.

www.westdorset.com

➕ M17 ℹ 11 Antelope Walk ☎ 01305 267992 🕓 Apr–Oct Mon–Sat 9–5, Sun 10–3; Oct–Apr Mon–Sat 9–4

EDEN PROJECT

A gateway into the world of plants, the Eden Project generates climates of the world inside two gigantic 'biodomes' – futuristic conservatories. Situated in a former clay quarry, the biodomes recreate different climates enabling visitors to wind their way through plants from places such as the Amazon, West Africa, Malaysia, the Mediterranean, South Africa and California.

www.edenproject.com

🚻 117 ✉ Bodelva, St Austell ☎ 01726 811911 🕙 Mar–Oct daily 10–4:30; Nov–Feb daily 10–3 💷 Expensive 🍴 Café (£)

EXETER

Although much rebuilt after bombing in World War II, Exeter has some attractive parts. The city's most distinguished feature is its cathedral, a superb architectural masterpiece enhanced by two great Norman towers that flank the nave. Inside you'll find the longest unbroken Gothic ceiling in the world, a stunning bishop's throne and misericords that are thought to be the oldest in the country, dating from 1260.

www.exeter.gov.uk

➕ K17

ℹ️ Dix's Field ☎ 01392 665700 🕓 Sep–Jun Mon–Sat 9–5; Jul–Aug Mon–Sat 9–5, Sun 10–4

EXMOOR

Best places to see, ➤ 40–41.

FROME

Lying at the eastern end of the Mendip Hills, Frome (pronounced 'froom') is a picturesque collection of steep cobbled streets,

weavers' cottages, Georgian houses, old shops and a thriving market. The town's prosperity was founded on cloth making, chiefly from the medieval period to the end of the 18th century. Catherine Hill and Gentle Street are worth exploring and the congregational chapel on Rook Lane is particularly fine.

www.frometouristinfo.co.uk

✚ M16

ℹ The Round Tower, 2 Bridge Street ☎ 01373 467271 ⊘ Mon–Sat 10–5

GLASTONBURY

Glastonbury was a centre of the early Christian church and lies at the heart of the mystical Isle of Avalon. Stories abound of the Holy Grail, King Arthur and the miraculous Glastonbury Thorn, said to have sprouted from the staff of Joseph of Arimathea. There are abbey ruins and a tower crowning the evocative Tor, a conical hill rising above the Somerset Levels, and an extraordinary range of shops catering for pagan cults. The area is particularly known for the popular summer music festival at nearby Pilton (➤ 186), which takes places in June. To the south, the Jacobean Montacute House, near Yeovil, displays important works from the National Portrait Gallery.

www.glastonburytic.co.uk

✚ M16

ℹ 9 High Street ☎ 01458 832954 ⊘ Apr–Oct Mon–Sat 10–5, Sun 11–5; Nov–Mar daily 10–4

GLOUCESTER

From Roman origins, Gloucester became a major port on the River Severn, until difficulties of navigation shifted the focus of trade to Bristol, substantially downstream. The docks, which had developed

following the opening of the Sharpness Canal in 1827, declined too, but in recent years have seen a revival, and are now a vigorous and vast commercial enterprise – especially if you're looking for antiques. The pride of Gloucester, however, is its enormous cathedral, which has huge Norman columns, and the tomb of Edward II. Gloucester's

lively streets are bustling with shops, pubs and businesses, but all are noticeably lower key than those at nearby Cheltenham.

www.gloucester.gov.uk/tourism

➕ B10

ℹ 28 Southgate Street ☎ 01452 396572 🕓 Mon 10–5, Tue–Sat 9:30–5; Jul–Aug Sun 11–3

ISLE OF WIGHT

Known locally as 'The Island', the Isle of Wight packs a great scenic punch. It has a mild climate, and though it is only just off the Hampshire coast, its remoteness has attracted many famous visitors, including Tennyson, Charles Dickens and Queen Victoria, who built a retreat for her family at **Osborne House,** and lived here after Prince Albert died. Not surprisingly, the island has a good deal of Victoriana, it also has beautiful, unspoiled countryside, much like southern England without the traffic, and a varied and impressive coastline, with chalk stacks (the Needles – best seen as you approach by ferry from France) and sandy beaches.

www.islandbreaks.co.uk

➕ N17

ℹ️ Guildhall, High Street, Newport ☎ 01983 813818 🕑 Mon–Sat 9:30–5, Sun 10–3:30; opening times Oct–Mar may vary, telephone for details

Osborne House

✉️ 1 mile (1.6km) east of Cowes

☎ 01983 200022 🕑 Apr–Sep daily 10–5; Oct daily 10–3; Nov–Mar Wed–Sun 10–3 👋 Expensive

LANHYDROCK HOUSE

Lanhydrock House is a fascinating late 19th-century house, full of period atmosphere and the trappings of a high Victorian country house. The gatehouse and north wing survive from the 17th century, but the rest of the house was rebuilt following a fire in 1881. The gardens are famously beautiful.

www.nationaltrust.org.uk

➕ H17 ✉️ Lanhydrock, near Bodmin

☎ 01208 265950 🕑 House: mid-Mar to Sep Tue–Sun 11–5; Oct Tue–Sun 11–4:30. Gardens: all year daily 10–5:30

👋 Moderate 🍴 Restaurant and café (£)

LONGLEAT

Longleat House is a vast Elizabethan mansion, with 19th-century interiors and numerous tourist attractions, not least lions, motion simulators, a railway and the world's longest hedge maze. The house has been the home of the Thynne (or Thynn) family for more than 450 years, and is now lived in by the 7th Marquess of Bath and his family. As well as providing visitor attractions, Longleat also plays an important role in the world programme of the breeding and conservation of endangered species.

www.longleat.co.uk

🚩 M16 ✉ Warminster ☎ 01985 844400 🕐 House: all year, daily. Safari Park: mid-Mar to early Nov; telephone for opening times ✋ Expensive 🍴 Cafés (£)

NEW FOREST NATIONAL PARK

The name of this vast special heritage area in southwest Hampshire is misleading. There is more heathland than woodland and it certainly isn't new. It's the remains of a primeval forest enclosed and protected by William the Conqueror, who used it as a deer-hunting reserve. Forest people still graze their animals and exercise ancient woodland rights that go back to the time of the Conquest. The main wooded area is around Lyndhurst, the so-called 'capital' of the Forest. In the south of the forest lies Beaulieu, a pretty village, most famous for the **National Motor Museum,** with over 250 historic vehicles.

www.newforestnpa.gov.uk

➕ N17 ℹ️ New Forest Visitor Information Centre, High Street, Lyndhurst

☎ 023 8028 2269 🕐 Daily 10–5

National Motor Museum

✉️ Beaulieu, Hampshire ☎ 01590 612345; www.beaulieu.co.uk

🕐 May–Sep daily 10–5:30; Oct–Apr daily 10–4:30

PORTSMOUTH

Occupying the peninsula of Portsea Island, Portsmouth is Britain's foremost naval base. The Romans were not slow to recognize the strategic importance of this position, and built a fortress, Portchester Castle (one of Britain's finest Roman sites), here. But it was only after the Norman Conquest that a peopled settlement developed, and not until Tudor times that the position was fully exploited. The Royal Naval Base on Queen Street is where you'll find the

Flagship Portsmouth, comprising HMS *Warrior* 1860, HMS *Victory*, the *Mary Rose*, the Royal Naval Museum, the Dockyard Apprentice exhibition and the Harbour Tour.

www.visitportsmouth.co.uk

➕ P17 ℹ️ The Hard, Portsmouth ☎ 023 9282 6722 🕐 Daily 9:30–5:15

Flagship Portsmouth

✉️ Historic Dockyard ☎ 023 9272 8060; www.historicdockyard.co.uk

🕐 Apr–Oct daily 10–4:30; Nov–Mar daily 10–4 ✋ Very expensive

ISLE OF PURBECK

Take the ferry from Sandbanks in Bournemouth, and this part of Dorset really feels like an island, jutting into Poole Harbour. No other coastline this near to London is as dramatic, and the coast path takes in switchback cliffs and geological wonders such as Lulworth Cove and the natural arch of Durdle Door. From the main town, Swanage, a steam railway heads to Corfe Castle, a village dominated by the jagged ruin of a medieval castle.

www.purbeck.gov.uk

✚ M17

🛈 Purbeck Information and Heritage Centre, South Street, Wareham
☎ 01929 552740 🕔 Easter–Oct Mon–Sat and Sun in school hols 9:30–5; Nov–Easter Mon–Sat 9:30–4

ST IVES

Beautifully positioned, with sandy beaches flanking a rugged headland, St Ives is a small town of cobbled streets and steep alleyways. Its prosperity was founded on pilchards and tin mining, but the town now relies on tourism and art, having attracted many well-known artists including Barbara Hepworth, Naum Gabo and Roger Hilton. The **Barbara Hepworth Museum and Sculpture Garden** gives a detailed insight into the local arts scene. The **Tate Gallery,** overlooking Porthmeor Beach, also shows local work.

www.visit-westcornwall.com

✚ G17 🛈 The Guildhall, Street-an-Pol ☎ 01736 796297 🕔 Early May to mid-Sep Mon–Fri 9–5, Sat 10–4, Sun 10–2; mid-Sep to early May Mon–Fri 9–5, Sat 10–1

Barbara Hepworth Museum and Sculpture Garden

✉ Barnoon Hill ☎ 01736 796226 🕔 Mar–Oct daily 10–5; Nov–Feb Tue–Sun 10–4 💷 Inexpensive

Tate Gallery

☎ 01736 796226; www.tate.org.uk/stives

🕐 Mar–Oct daily 10–5; Nov–Feb
Tue–Sun 10–4 ✋ Moderate 🍴 Café (£)

SALISBURY

England's finest cathedral city has
grown since 1220, when the
settlement moved from Old Sarum.
The cathedral, with its huge spire,
was begun in 1220 and is entirely
Early English in style. It is one of
the finest medieval buildings in the
country, and the Chapter House
contains a copy of the Magna Carta.
The city of Salisbury itself is a
mixture of medieval, Georgian and
Victorian buildings, with no high-rise
buildings to challenge the
dominance of the cathedral.

www.visitwiltshire.com

✚ N16 🛈 Fish Row ☎ 01722 334956
🕐 Oct–Apr Mon–Sat 9:30–5; May
Mon–Sat 9:30–5, Sun 10:30–4:30;
Jun–Sep Mon–Sat 9:30–6, Sun
10:30–4:30

STONEHENGE

Best places to see, ➤ 48–49.

TRURO

The county town of Cornwall was the main port for the export of tin, and became a medieval 'stannary' town, where tin was taken to be weighed and taxed. Little remains of Truro's ancient past, though there are numerous fine Georgian buildings, especially along Lemon Street. Completed in 1910, the cathedral was the first Anglican cathedral to be built since St Paul's in London, and incorporates parts of the earlier church that stood on the site.
www.truro.gov.uk

➕ H17 ℹ Municipal Building, Boscawen Street ☎ 01872 274555
🕐 Apr–Oct Mon–Fri 9–5:30, Sat 9–5; Nov–Mar Mon–Fri 9–5

WELLS

The exquisite market place in this, England's smallest city, seems to have architecture from every conceivable period, including two medieval gatehouses, one of which leads to the cathedral, the other to the Bishop's Palace.

The city seems to have altered little in 800 years, having successfully hung on to its medieval character, and is perfect for a relaxing day, or as a base from which to visit the Mendip Hills and Cheddar Gorge (➤ 168).

The cathedral, one of England's most beautiful, dates from the 12th century, and its most impressive feature is the ornate west front, although many visitors are fascinated by the mechanical clock dating from 1392, high up in the north transept. Cathedral Close is a cluster of attractive buildings with histories closely associated with the cathedral. A year-round programme of recitals provides the opportunity to hear a cathedral choir in full song.

www.wells.gov.uk
✚ M16 🛈 Town Hall, Market Place
☎ 01749 672552 ⏱ Apr–Sep
Mon–Sat 9:30–5:30, Sun 10–4; Oct
Mon–Sat 10–5, Sun 10–4; Nov–Mar
Mon–Sat 10–4

WINCHESTER

Alfred the Great's Wessex capital was the capital of all England from the 10th century until the Norman Conquest. Twenty kings are buried here and it overflows with medieval and later buildings. So important was the city in the 11th century that William the Conqueror's coronation was held both in London and Winchester. It was the monks of Winchester that he commissioned to carry out his Domesday Survey. Winchester also enjoys literary links: Jane Austen lived at nearby Chawton and died in the city in 1817, and pioneer angler Isaak Walton also died here in 1653.

www.visitwinchester.co.uk
✚ N16 🛈 Guildhall, The Broadway
☎ 01962 840500 ⏱ Apr–Sep
Mon–Sat 9:30–5:30, Sun 11–4;
Oct–Mar Mon–Sat 10–5

a walk around the Lizard

A challenging walk through spectacular coastal scenery with lunch in a picturesque fishing village.

Head towards the lighthouse and soon go into the grounds of the youth hostel, heading for the cliff path. Turn left along the path and follow it to Housel Bay. Continue round Bass Point.

The disused castellated building here was once a signal station.

At Kilcobben Cove go behind the lifeboat station and into Church Cove.

On the beach is a lifeboat station built at the end of the 19th century in such a way that the lifeboat had to be turned around 90 degrees before it could be launched; it didn't last.

Follow the coastal path to the Devil's Frying Pan, a large, collapsed cave, and go round the back of it to Inglewidden. Continue with the coastal path to Cadgwith, and go through the gardens of Hillside.

Cadgwith is a charming village on steep sea slopes, with lots of thatched cottages and buildings in the serpentine rock for which the Lizard is famous.

Go back up to Hillside, but turn right in Prazegooth Lane. At the top, bear right to a road. Turn left, pass Gwavas

Jersey Farm and, when the road bends right, go forward onto a footpath. Head across a field to a marker pole, and up steps onto the top of a wall. At the other end take a concrete farm access road to Trethvas Farm, and turn left for the Lizard. Continue now across fields to the Lizard, and then head for the 'Most Southerly Point'. In so doing you will return to your starting point.

Distance 7.5 miles (12km)
Time 5 hours with stops, 3–4 hours without stopping
Start/end point Lizard lighthouse car park ✚ G18
Lunch Cadgwith Cove Inn (£–££)

HOTELS

The Ayrlington (££)

An elegant Victorian villa within a few minutes' walk of the Roman Baths and the city centre. The hotel, which overlooks the medieval abbey, offers an extensive range of facilities.

✉ 24–25 Pulteney Road, Bath ☎ 01225 425495; www.ayrlington.com

Bovey Castle Hotel (££–£££)

See page 72.

Hatton Court (£–££)

Set 600ft (183m) above sea level on top of Upton Hill, this manor house provides sweeping views across the River Severn to the Malvern Hills. The emphasis here is on comfort.

✉ Upton Hill, Upton St Leonards, Gloucester ☎ 01452 617412

The Idle Rocks Hotel (££)

With commanding views over the quayside in St Mawes, this comfortable Cornish retreat is excellently placed for local walks and has a good restaurant.

✉ Harbourside, St Mawes, Cornwall ☎ 0844 502 7587

Pedn Olva (££)

A comfortable, relaxed hotel, with an excellent restaurant.

✉ The Warren, West Porthminster Beach, St Ives, Cornwall
☎ 01736 796222; www.pednolva.co.uk

Stock Hill Country House Hotel (£££)

The hotel, which also boasts an outstanding restaurant, stands in 11 acres (4.5ha) of parkland and is surrounded by rare old trees. Charm and detailed elegance are the hallmark of all the rooms.

✉ Stock Hill, Gillingham, Dorset ☎ 01747 823626

Thistle Bristol (££)

Though very centrally situated, this refurbished hotel offers quiet accommodation and all modern amenities.

✉ Broad Street, Bristol ☎ 0870 333 9130; www.thistle.com/hotels/bristol

RESTAURANTS

Castle Hotel (££)
The Castle is something of a gastronomic institution in Somerset.
✉ Castle Green, Taunton, Somerset ☎ 01823 272671 ⏲ Mon–Sat lunch, dinner; Sun lunch only

Le Champignon Sauvage (£££)
Classic cooking from David Everitt-Matthias.
✉ 24–26 Suffolk Road, Cheltenham, Gloucestershire ☎ 01242 573449
⏲ Tue–Sat lunch, dinner

Fifteen Cornwall (££)
Jamie Oliver's charitable venture has come to the seaside.
✉ Watergate Bay, Cornwall ☎ 01637 861000 ⏲ Daily 8:30–10, 12–2:30, 6.15–9.15

George & Dragon (££)
Award-winning pub specializing in fresh fish.
✉ High Street, Rowde, Wiltshire ☎ 01380 723053 ⏲ Tue–Sat 12–3, 7–10; Sun 12–4

The New Angel (££–£££)
John Burton Race's restaurant is popular for his skilful cooking and seasonal, locally sourced produce.
✉ 2 South Embankment, Dartmouth, Devon ☎ 01803 839425 ⏲ Tue 6:30–9:30; Wed–Sat 9–11, 12–2:30, 6:30–9:30; Sun 9–11, 12–2:30

The Old Success Inn (£–££)
See page 58.

Pump Room (££)
See page 59.

Riverstation (££)
A fine restaurant on the first floor and a bar kitchen at dock level.
✉ The Grove, Bristol ☎ 0117 914 4434 ⏲ Bar kitchen: meals all day. Restaurant: daily 12–2:30 (Sun 12–3), 6–10:30 (Fri, Sat 6–11, Sun 6–9)

The Seafood Restaurant (££–£££)

Rick Stein's popular restaurant is the place to go for inventive seafood. Non-fish options are also available.

✉ Padstow, Cornwall ☎ 01841 532700 ⏱ Daily 12–2:30, 6:30–10

Tanners Restaurant (£££)

A 15th-century house where Pilgrim Fathers ate their final meal in England. The modern menu has French and American influences.

✉ Prysten House, Finewell Street, Plymouth, Devon ☎ 01752 252001
⏱ Lunch, dinner Tue–Sat

ENTERTAINMENT

Colston Hall

Bristol's main venue for classical and popular music.

✉ Colston Street, Bristol ☎ 0117 922 3686; www.colstonhall.org

Everyman Theatre

Produces many shows from Shakespeare to stand-up comedy.

✉ Regent Street, Cheltenham, Gloucestershire ☎ 01242 572573;
www.everymantheatre.org.uk

Exeter Phoenix

Thought-provoking drama, dance, live art and music productions.

✉ Bradninch Place, Gandy Street, Exeter, Devon ☎ 01392 667080;
www.exeterphoenix.org.uk

Glastonbury

Renowned for its music festival at the end of June in nearby Pilton.

☎ 0844 412 4626; www.glastonburyfestivals.co.uk

Minack Theatre

Outdoor theatre, musicals and opera in a spectacular clifftop setting.

✉ Porthcurno, Cornwall ☎ 01736 810181; www.minack.com

Theatre Royal

Drama and ballet are regularly featured at the Theatre Royal.

✉ Sawclose, Bath ☎ 01225 448844; www.theatreroyal.org.uk

Sight Locator Index

This index relates to the maps on the covers. We have given map references to the main sights of interest in the book. Grid references in italics indicate sights featured on the town plan. Some sights within towns may not be plotted on the maps.

Alnwick Castle **D2**
Avebury **N16**
Bath **M16**
Berwick-Upon-Tweed **C1**
Birmingham **C9**
Blenheim Palace **P15**
Blickling Hall **T13**
Bodiam Castle **R17**
Bridgnorth **B9**
Brighton **Q17**
Bristol **M15**
British Museum *London d1*
Buckingham Palace
  London b4
Buckland Abbey **J17**
Bury St Edmunds **F10**
Buxton **C7**
Cambridge **E10**
Canterbury **S16**
Carlisle **B3**
Castle Howard **D5**
Castleton **C7**
Chartwell **R16**
Chatsworth House **C7**
Cheddar Gorge **L16**
Cheltenham **B10**
Chester **B7**
The Chilterns **P15**
Cotehele House **J17**
Cotswolds **N15**
Covent Garden *London e2*
Dartmoor **K17**
Docklands *London h2*
  (off map)
Dorchester **M17**
Dover Castle **S17**
Durham **D4**
Eden Project **H17**
Eden Valley **B4**
Ely **E9**
Exeter **K17**
Exmoor **K16**
Fountains Abbey **C5**
Frome **M16**
Glastonbury **M16**
Gloucester **B10**
Greenwich *London h3*
  (off map)
Haddon Hall **C7**

Hadrian's Wall **C3**
Hastings **R17**
Haworth **C6**
Hebden Bridge **C6**
Hereford **A10**
Hever Castle **R16**
Holy Island **D1**
Hyde Park *London a4*
  (off map)
Ironbridge Gorge **B8**
Isle of Purbeck **M17**
Isle of Wight **N17**
Kendal **B4**
Kenilworth Castle **C9**
Lake District **B4**
Lancaster **B5**
Lanhydrock House **H17**
Leeds **C6**
Leeds Castle **R16**
Levens Hall and Topiary
  Gardens **B5**
Lichfield **C8**
Lincoln **E7**
Liverpool **A6**
London **Q16**
London Eye *London c4*
Longleat **M16**
Ludlow **B9**
Lullingstone Roman Villa **R16**
Lyme Park **C7**
Malvern **B10**
Manchester **B6**
Much Wenlock **B8**
Museum of London
  London h1
National Coal Mining Museum
  C6
National Gallery *London d3*
Natural History Museum
  London a4 (off map)
New Forest National Park **N17**
Newcastle upon Tyne **D3**
Norfolk Broads **T13**
North of England Open Air
  Museum, Beamish **C3**
North York Moors **D4**
Norwich **T13**
Nottingham **D8**
Oxford **P15**

Palace of Westminster
  London d5
Penshurst Place **R16**
Portsmouth **P17**
Quarry Bank Mill, Styal **B7**
Richmond **C4**
Royal Botanic Gardens, Kew
  Q16
Rye **R17**
Saffron Walden **E10**
St Albans **Q15**
St Ives **G17**
St Paul's Cathedral
  London h2
Salisbury **N16**
Saltaire **C6**
Science Museum *London a4*
  (off map)
Seven Sisters **R17**
Sherwood Forest **D7**
Shrewsbury **B8**
Sizergh Castle **B5**
Skipton **C5**
Stoke-on-Trent **B7**
Stonehenge **N16**
Stratford-upon-Avon **C9**
Suffolk Coast and Heaths **T14**
Tate Britain *London d6*
Tate Modern *London h3*
Tatton Park **B7**
Tower of London *London h2*
  (off map)
Trafalgar Square *London d3*
Truro **H17**
Victoria and Albert Museum
  London a4 (off map)
Walmer Castle **S16**
Warwick Castle **C9**
The Weald **R17**
Wells **M16**
Westminster Abbey
  London d5
Whitby **E4**
Winchester **N16**
Windsor **Q16**
Woburn Abbey **D10**
Worcester **B9**
York **D6**
Yorkshire Dales **C5**

Index

Abbot Hall Art Gallery 104
accommodation 72–73, 92–93, 114–115, 138–139, 162–163, 184
activities 66–67
airports 26
Albert Dock 106
Aldeburgh 156
Alexander Keiller Museum 166
Alnwick Castle 98
Ambleside 45
American Museum of Decorative Art 37
Appleby-in-Westmorland 24, 100
Areas of Outstanding Natural Beauty (AONB) 11
Ashmolean Museum 47
Audley End House 64
Avebury 67, 166

banks 32
Barbara Hepworth Museum and Sculpture Garden 178
Bath 36–37
Battle Abbey 148–149
Beamish 108
Berwick-upon-Tweed 98–99
Bibury 39
Big Ben 85
Birmingham 118
Blenheim Palace 119
Blickling Hall 142
Bodiam Castle 143
Bodleian Library 47
Bolton Priory 54
Bourton-on-the-Water 39
Bowness 45
breakdowns 27
breath-testing 27
Bridgnorth 119
Brighton 143
Bristol 166–167
British Museum 78
Broadway 39
Brockhole 45
Brontë Parsonage Museum 102
Buckingham Palace 78–79
Buckland Abbey 167
Bury St Edmunds 144
buses and coaches 29
Buxton 120

Cadgwith 182
Cambridge 144–145
Canterbury 145
Captain Cook Memorial Museum 113

car rental 29
Carlisle 99
Castle Howard 100
Castlerigg 67
Castleton 120–121
Central England 117–140
Chartwell 146
Chatsworth House 121
Cheddar Gorge 168
Cheltenham 168–169
Chester 122
children's entertainment 60–61
The Chilterns 146–147
Chipping Camden 39
Cirencester 39
Clifton Suspension Bridge 167
climate and seasons 22
Clumber Park 65, 130
Corfe Castle 178
Cotehele House 169
Cotswolds 38–39
Covent Garden 79
credit cards 30–31
currency and foreign exchange 30

Dartmoor 170
Darwin, Charles 132
dental treatment 23
Derwent Water 45
Docklands 80
Dorchester 170
Dover Castle 147
drinking water 32
drive
   South Downs 160–161
driving 22, 27
drugs and medicines 32
Dunkery Beacon 40
Durdle Door 178
Durham 100

eating out 58–59, 93–94, 115–116, 139–140, 163–164, 185–186
Eden Project 171
Eden Valley 100
1853 Gallery 111
electricity 31
Ely 148
embassies and consulates 31
emergency telephone numbers 31
entertainment 96, 116, 140, 164, 186
Eton 158
Eureka! 60

Exeter 172
Exmoor 40–41

fares and tickets 29
Fashion Museum 37
ferries 26
festivals and events 24–25
Fitzwilliam Museum 145
Flambards Experience 60
food and drink 12–15
   see also eating out
Fountains Abbey 101
Frome 172–173
fuel 27

Gardens of the Rose 155
Gladstone Pottery Museum 133
Glastonbury 173
Gloucester 174
Grasmere 45
Grassington 54
Greenwich 80

Haddon Hall 123
Hadrian's Wall 42–43
Hampton Court Palace 64
Hardwick Hall 64
Harlow Carr Botanical Garden 65
Hastings 148–149
Hawes 55
Haworth 102
health and safety 32
health insurance 22, 23
Hebden Bridge 102–103
Hereford 123
Hever Castle 149
Holy Island 103
Houses of Parliament 85
Housesteads Fort and Musuem 43
Hyde Park 69, 81

Iping 161
Ironbridge Gorge 19, 124–125
Isle of Purbeck 178
Isle of Wight 174–175

Jorvik Viking Centre 52, 53

Kendal 45, 104
Kenilworth Castle 125
Keswick 45
Laing Gallery 108
Lake District 18, 44–45
Lancaster 104–105
language 33

Lanhydrock House 175
Lathkill Dale 136–137
Leeds 105
Leeds Castle 150
Legoland Windsor 60
Levens Hall and Topiary Gardens
   106
Leyburn 55
Lichfield 125
Lincoln 126
Lindisfarne Priory and Museum
   103
Liverpool 106–107
Lizard 182–183
London 77–96
London Eye 82
Longleat 176
Lost Gardens of Heligan 65
Ludlow 126–127
Lullingstone Roman Villa 150
Lulworth Cove 178
Lyme Park 127
Lynmouth 40
Lynton 40

Madame Tussaud's 61
Magna 61
Malham Cove 54
Malvern 128
Manchester 107
Midhurst 161
Minsmere 156
money 30
Montacute House 173
Morwellham Quay 170
Much Wenlock 128
Museum of London 82

National Coal Mining Museum
   108
National Gallery 82–83
national holidays 24–25
National Maritime Museum 61
National Motor Museum
   176–177
National Parks 11
National Railway Museum 53
National Sea Life Centre 118
Natural History Museum 84
New Forest National Park
   176–177
Newcastle upon Tyne 108
Norfolk Broads 150–151
North of England Open Air
   Museum, Beamish 108
North York Moors 110
Northern England 97–116

Northleach 39
Norwich 152
Nottingham 129

opening hours 32
Osborne House 175
Oxford 46–47

Palace of Westminster 85
Parsonage Museum 102
passports and visas 22
Pennine Way National Trail 55
Penshurst Place 152–153
Petworth House and Park 64
Peveril Castle 120–121
pharmacies 32
Pittville Pump Room 168
police 31
Poole's Cavern 120
Portsmouth 177
postal services 31
public transport 28–29
pubs 62–63

Quarry Bank Mill, Styal 130

Richmond 55, 111
Roman Baths Museum 36–37
Royal Botanic Gardens, Kew 85
Rydal 45
Rye 153

Saffron Walden 154
St Albans 154–155
St Ives 178
St Martins-in-the-Fields 88–89
St Paul's Cathedral 86
Salisbury 179
Saltaire 111
Samuel Johnson Birthplace
   Museum 125
Science Museum 86–87
seat belts 27
Serpentine Gallery 81
Settle–Carlisle Railway 99
Seven Sisters 155
Severn Valley Railway 119
Shakespeare, William 133
Sherwood Forest 130
shopping 95
Shrewsbury 132
Sizergh Castle 112
Skipton 55, 112–113
Snowshill 39
South Downs 160–161
Southeast England 141–164
Southwest England 165–186

speed limits 27
Speedwell Cavern 61
Stanton 39
Stoke-on-Trent 132–133
Stokesay Castle 127
Stonehenge 48–49
Stratford-upon-Avon 133
Studley Royal Water Garden 101
Suffolk Coast and Heaths 156
Swanage 178

Tate Britain 87
Tate Gallery, St Ives 178–179
Tate Modern 88
Tatton Park 134
taxis 29
telephones 31
time differences 23
tipping 30
tourist offices 23, 30
Tower of London 50–51
Trafalgar Square 88–89
trains 26, 28–29
Truro 180
Tullie House Museum and Art
   Gallery 99

Upper and Lower Slaughter 39
Urbis 107

Valley of the Rocks 40
Victoria and Albert Museum
   90–91

Walker Art Gallery 107
walks 70–71
   Lathkill Dale 136–137
   Lizard 182–183
   London's Royal Parks 68–69
Walmer Castle 157
Warwick Castle 134
Watersmeet 41
The Weald 157
websites 23
Wells 180–181
Wenlock Priory 128
Westminster Abbey 91
Westonbirt Arboretum 65
Whitby 113
Winchester 181
Windermere 44–45
Windsor 158
Woburn Abbey 158
Worcester 135

York 52–53
Yorkshire Dales 54–55

Acknowledgements

The Automobile Association would like to thank the following photographers, companies and picture libraries for their assistance in the preparation of this book. Abbreviations for the picture credits are as follows: (t) top; (b) bottom; (c) centre; (l) left; (r) right; (AA) AA World Travel Library

4l Malvern Hills, AA/H Palmer; **4c** Lord Mayor's Parade, AA/P Enticknap; **4r** York Minster, AA/P Bennett; **5l** Gravetye Manor, AA/T Souter; **5r** Hyde Park, AA/R Strange; **6/7** Malvern Hills, AA/H Palmer; **8/9** Castle Howard, AA/J Morrison; **10** Houses of Parliament, AA/W Voysey; **10/11t** Buckland in the Moor, AA/R Moss; **10/11c** Carlisle Cathedral, AA/P Bennett; **11bl** Woburn Safari Park, AA/M Birkitt; **11cr** Wedgwood Visitor Centre, AA/P Baker; **12c** Portland, AA/M Jourdan; **12bl** Cheddar Gorge Cheese Co., AA/C Jones; **12/13t** Branscombe, AA/P Baker; **12/13b** Sweetings Oyster Bar, AA/R Mort; **13** Cup of tea, Stockbyte Royalty Free Photos; **14** Covent Garden, AA/M Jourdan; **15cl** Bottle of wine & glasses, Stockbyte Royalty Free Photos; **15cr** Ritz Tea Rooms, AA; **16** Black cab, AA/M Jourdan; **16/17** Lincoln Cathedral, AA/C Coe; **18/19** Trooping the Colour, AA/T Woodcock; **19** Enginuity Museum, Ironbridge, AA/M Haywood; **20/21**, Lord Mayor's Parade, AA/P Enticknap; **24** Obby Oss Festival, Padstow, AA/J Wood; **25** Cowes Week, AA/W Voysey; **26** Eurostar train, AA/W Voysey; **26/27** Stanstead Airport, AA/J Miller; **28** Bus, Oxford Street, AA/M Jourdan; **29** Liverpool Street Station, AA/R Strange; **34/35** York Minster, AA/P Bennett; **36** Roman Baths & Bath Abbey, AA/M Birkitt; **36/37** Bath, AA/S&O Mathews; **38** Lower Slaughter, AA/K Doran; **38/39** Bibury, AA/T Souter; **40cl** Exmoor Animal Centre, AA/W Voysey; **40bl** Lynmouth, AA/C Jones; **41t** Dulverton, AA/A Lawson; **41b** Valley of the Rocks, AA/C Jones; **42/43** Housesteads, AA/C Lees; **43** Vercovicium, AA/T Mackie; **44/45** Ashness Bridge, AA/T Mackie; **45** Loughrigg Fell, AA/T Mackie; **46** Radcliffe Camera, AA/S&O Mathews; **46/47** Oxford, AA/A Lawson; **47** Ashmolean Museum, AA/S Day; **48/49** Stonehenge, AA; **50/51t** Tower of London, AA/S Gibson; **50/51b** Tower of London, AA/W Voysey; **52** York Minster, AA/W Voysey; **52/53** National Railway Museum, AA/R Newton; **53** York, AA/R Newton; **54** Linton Falls, AA/A Baker; **54/55** Pennine Way, AA/AJ Hopkins; **55** Wharfedale, AA; **56/57**, Gravetye Manor, AA/T Souter; **59** Bath Pump Room, AA/E Meacher; **61** Norfolk Wildlife Park, AA/H Williams; **62** Elterwater, AA/EA Bowness; **64/65** Hampton Court, AA/R Mort; **66/67** Coniston Water, AA/M Birkitt; **68** Hyde Park, AA/R Strange; **70** Taunton, AA/R Hall; **70tr** Buttermere Lake, Lake District, AA/T Mackie; **70cr** Limestone pavement, Malham Cove, AA/T Mackie; **70b** White Cliffs, East Sussex, AA/J Miller; **71t** View over Wye Valley from Yat Rock, Herefordshire, AA/H Williams; **71b** Wicken Fen, AA/T Mackie; **72** Dorchester Hotel, AA/P Wilson; **73** Ludlow, AA/I Burgum; **74/75** Hyde Park, AA/R Strange; **77** Buckingham Palace, AA/M Jourdan; **78** British Museum, AA/M Jourdan; **79t** The Mall, AA/T Woodcock; **79b** Covent Garden, AA/M Trelawny; **80** Dome of Old Royal Naval College, Greenwich, AA/N Setchfield; **80/81** Hyde Park, AA/R Mort; **82tl** London Eye, AA/M Jourdan; **82c** Museum of London, AA/T Woodcock; **82/83** National Gallery, AA; **84/85** Natural History Museum, AA/ M Jourdan; **85** Royal Botanical Gardens Kew, AA/T Woodcock; **86** Science Museum, AA/J Tims; **86/87** St Paul's Cathedral, AA/T Woodcock; **87** Tate Gallery, AA/P Wilson; **88/89** Trafalgar Square, AA/J McMillan; **90/91** Victoria and Albert Museum, AA/G Wrona; **91** Westminster Abbey, AA/B Smith; **97** Hebden Bridge, AA/L Whitwam; **98** Alnwick Castle, AA/C Lees; **99** Carlisle, AA/P Bennett; **100/101** Fountains Abbey, AA/L Whitwam; **102** Haworth, AA/P Wilson; **102/103** Lindisfarne Castle, AA/C Lees; **104/105** Killhope Lead Mining Museum, AA/C Lees; **105** Leeds and Liverpool Canal, AA/T Marsh; **106** Liverpool, AA; **106/107** Levens Hall, AA/T Mackie; **107** Manchester, AA/C Molyneux; **108/109** North of England Open Air Museum, AA/J Beazley; **110** Sutton Bank, North York Moors National Park, AA/M Kipling; **111** Castle, Richmond, AA/P Baker; **112** Skipton, AA/P Wilson; **112/113** Whitby, AA/R Newton; **117** Warwick Castle, AA; **118** Birmingham City Museum and Art Gallery, AA/V Greaves; **118/119** Blenheim Palace, AA; **119** Bridgnorth, AA/I Burgum; **120** Buxton, AA/P Baker; **120/121** Peak Cavern, AA/M Birkitt; **122** Chester, AA/C Jones; **122/123** Haddon Hall, AA/P Baker; **123** Hereford Cathedral, AA; **124** Ironbridge, AA/M Haywood; **126** Ludlow, AA/R Surman; **126/127** Ludlow Castle, AA/C Jones; **127** Lyme Park, AA/M Birkitt; **128t** Malvern Priory, AA/C Jones; **128b** Wenlock Priory, AA/M Short; **128/129** Nottingham, AA/P Baker; **131** Sherwood Forest, AA/M Birkitt; **132** St Chads Church Shrewsbury, AA/C Jones; **132/133** Shrewsbury, AA/M Allwood-Coppin; **133** Stratford upon Avon, AA/J Wyand; **134/135** Tatton Park, AA; **135** Worcester, AA/S&O Mathews; **136/137** Bakewell, AA/P Baker; **141** Mathematical Bridge, Cambridge, AA/M Moody; **142/143** Blickling Hall, AA; **143t** Bodiam Castle, AA/J Miller; **143b** Brighton, AA/P Brown; **144** Bury St Edmunds, AA/R Surman; **144/145** Cambridge, AA/M Birkitt; **146/147t** Chartwell, AA/P Baker; **146/147b** Midhurst, AA/S&O Mathews; **147** Dover Castle, AA/D Forss; **148** Ely Cathedral, AA/T Mackie; **148/149** Hastings, AA/W Voysey; **150t** Leeds Castle, AA/D Forss; **150c** Lullingstone, AA/S&O Mathews; **150/151** Norfolk Broads National Park, AA/A Baker; **152** Norwich Cathedral, AA/S&O Mathews; **152/153** Norwich, AA/T Souter; **154** Saffron Walden, AA/C Coe; **154/155** Seven Sisters, AA/C Coe; **156/157** Minsmere, AA/H Williams; **156** Southwold AA/T Mackie; **157** Weald and Downland Open Air Museum, AA/J Miller; **158/159** Windsor, AA/W Voysey; **160/161** The Ridgeway Hackpen Hill, AA/B Johnson; **165** Hound Tor Dartmoor National Park, AA/P Baker; **166** Avebury, AA/W Voysey; **166/167** Clifton Suspension Bridge, AA/T Souter; **167** SS Great Britain Bristol, AA/S Day; **168/169** Cheddar Gorge, AA/S&O Mathews; **169** Cotehele Mill, AA/A Lawson; **170** Dartmoor, AA/W Voysey; **170/171** Eden Project, AA/R Tenison; **172** Frome, AA/R Moss; **172/173** Glastonbury Tor, AA/C Jones; **174** Gloucester Cathedral, AA/S Day; **174/175** The Needles, AA/S McBride; **175** Lanhydrock House, AA/R Moss; **176c** Longleat Safari Park, AA/W Voysey; **176b** New Forest ponies, AA/T Souter; **176/177** Longleat, AA/S Day; **177** HMS Victory Portsmouth, AA/W Voysey, **178/179** Flying Scotsman Swanage, AA/D Jackson; **179c** Salisbury Cathedral, AA/ C Jones; **179t** Salisbury Cathedral, AA/S&O Mathews; **180** Wells Cathedral, S&O Mathews; **180/181** Winchester Cathedral, AA/S Day; **182/183** Lizard Point, AA/C Jones.

Every effort has been made to trace the copyright holders, and we apologise in advance for any accidental errors. We would be happy to apply any corrections in the following edition of this publication.